Bloom's

GUIDES

William Golding's
Lord of the Flies
New Edition

The Adventures of Huckleberry Finn
All the Pretty Horses
Animal Farm
The Autobiography of Malcolm X
The Awakening
The Bell Jar
Beloved
Beowulf
Black Boy
The Bluest Eye
Brave New World
The Canterbury Tales
Catch-22
The Catcher in the Rye
The Chosen
The Crucible
Cry, the Beloved Country
Death of a Salesman
Fahrenheit 451
A Farewell to Arms
Frankenstein
The Glass Menagerie
The Grapes of Wrath
Great Expectations
The Great Gatsby
Hamlet
The Handmaid's Tale
Heart of Darkness
The House on Mango Street
I Know Why the Caged Bird Sings
The Iliad
Invisible Man
Jane Eyre

The Joy Luck Club
The Kite Runner
Lord of the Flies
Macbeth
Maggie: A Girl of the Streets
The Member of the Wedding
The Metamorphosis
Native Son
Night
1984
The Odyssey
Oedipus Rex
Of Mice and Men
One Hundred Years of Solitude
Pride and Prejudice
Ragtime
A Raisin in the Sun
The Red Badge of Courage
Romeo and Juliet
The Scarlet Letter
A Separate Peace
Slaughterhouse-Five
Snow Falling on Cedars
The Stranger
A Streetcar Named Desire
The Sun Also Rises
A Tale of Two Cities
Their Eyes Were Watching God
The Things They Carried
To Kill a Mockingbird
Uncle Tom's Cabin
The Waste Land
Wuthering Heights

Bloom's
GUIDES

William Golding's
Lord of the Flies
New Edition

Edited & with an Introduction
by Harold Bloom

BLOOM'S
LITERARY CRITICISM
An imprint of Infobase Publishing

Bloom's Guides: Lord of the Flies—New Edition

Copyright © 2010 by Infobase Publishing

Introduction © 2010 by Harold Bloom

Bloom's Literary Criticism

An imprint of Infobase Publishing

132 West 31st Street

New York NY 10001

Library of Congress Cataloging-in-Publication Data

William Golding's Lord of the flies / edited and with an introduction by Harold Bloom. — New ed.

    p. cm. — (Bloom's guides)

    Includes bibliographical references and index.

    ISBN 978-1-60413-814-6 (hardcover : alk. paper) 1. Golding, William, 1911–1993. Lord of the flies. 2. Survival after airplane accidents, shipwrecks, etc., in literature. I. Bloom, Harold.

    PR6013.O35L65 2010

    823'.914—dc22

                2010001315

Bloom's Literary Criticism books are available at special discounts when purchased in bulk quantities for businesses, associations, institutions, or sales promotions. Please call our Special Sales Department in New York at (212) 967–8800 or (800) 322–8755.

You can find Bloom's Literary Criticism on the World Wide Web at http://www.chelseahouse.com

Contributing editor: Portia Williams Weiskel

Cover designed by Takeshi Takahashi

Composition by IBT Global, Troy NY

Cover printed by IBT Global, Troy NY

Book printed and bound by IBT Global, Troy NY

Date printed: May 2010

Printed in the United States of America

10 9 8 7 6 5 4 3 2 1

This book is printed on acid-free paper.

Contents

Introduction

HAROLD BLOOM

The survival of *Lord of the Flies* (1954), more than a half century after its initial publication, is not in itself a testimony to the book's permanence, even as a popular fiction of the boy's adventure story genre. William Golding, a schoolmaster for many years, clearly knew a good deal about the psychology of young boys, particularly in regard to group dynamics. Whether the psychological representations of *Lord of the Flies* remain altogether convincing seems to me rather questionable; the saintly Simon strains credibility as a naturalistic portrait. In many ways the book is remarkably tendentious and too clearly has a program to urge on us. Overt moral allegory, even in a lively adventure story, may arouse our resentments, and I find it difficult to reread *Lord of the Flies* without a certain skepticism toward Golding's designs on his reader. In some sense, the book is Mark Twain turned upside down, and I mean the Mark Twain of *Roughing It* rather than of *Adventures of Huckleberry Finn*. Sometimes I like to try the critical experiment of pretending to be Mark Twain as I read *Lord of the Flies*. How *would* Huck Finn have reacted to the regressive saga of the English schoolboys of *Lord of the Flies*? We cannot find any trace of Huck in Ralph or in Jack, in Simon or in Piggy or in Roger. Golding, I think, would have been furious at my suggestion that this has something to do with Huck's being American and Golding's boys being British. Original Sin is not a very American idea, and the wonderful skepticism of Huck, at any age, would have preserved him from being either an implausible saint or a bestial hunter. This is hardly to suggest that we are less savage or violence-prone than the British; Huck knows better, and we know better. But it may indicate some of the limitations of *Lord of the Flies*; as a grim fable, unrelieved in its rigor, it lacks all humor and is an involuntary parody of Twain's *Roughing It* or his *Innocents Abroad*.

Golding once said that the dead parachutist in *Lord of the Flies* was meant to represent "History," in the adult sense. The moral implication that Golding intended doubtless was that the group reversion to organized savagery in his book was no different from adult reversion, at any time. Whether a reader finds this convincing seems to me quite disputable: An American might want to reply, with Ralph Waldo Emerson, that there is no history, only biography. Golding's fable is vivid and is narrated with great skill, but is it a fable of universal relevance? At the end, Golding tells us that "Ralph wept for the end of innocence, the darkness of man's heart." Are we moved by Ralph's weeping, or do we flinch at it because of Golding's inverted sentimentalism? Emotion in excess of the object that provokes it tends to be a pragmatic definition of sentimentality. I suspect that it comes down to the issue of universalism: Do the boys of *Lord of the Flies* represent the human condition, or do they reflect the traditions of British schools with their restrictive structures, sometimes brutal discipline, and not always benign visions of human nature? Golding himself said that society, whether in life or in *Lord of the Flies*, plays only a minor role in bringing about human violence and depravity. But what about the one society his boys truly have known, the society of their schools? One can admire *Lord of the Flies* as a tale of adventure while wondering whether its moral fable was not far more insular than Golding seems to have realized.

Biographical Sketch

William Gerald Golding was born on September 19, 1911, to Mildred Golding, an activist for women's suffrage, and Alec Golding, a mathematics teacher and eventual senior master at Marlborough Grammar School. Golding led a somewhat isolated childhood, spent largely in the company of his nurse, Lily. He attended Marlborough Grammar School and, in 1930, he entered Brasenose College, Oxford, to study science but soon switched to English literature. While at college, a friend sent 29 of Golding's poems to Macmillan; his *Poems* was published in the Contemporary Poets series. In 1935, he received a B.A. in English and a diploma in education from Oxford and then became a social worker at a London settlement house. Golding wrote, acted, and produced for a small, noncommercial theater in London in his spare time. In 1939, he married Ann Brookfield, an analytical chemist; they had a son and a daughter. The same year he was married, Golding began teaching English, Greek literature in translation, and philosophy at Bishop Wordsworth's School in Salisbury. He was also involved in adult education, teaching in army camps and at Maidstone Gaol.

Golding enlisted in the Royal Navy at the start of World War II. He achieved the rank of lieutenant and was given command of a small rocket-launching craft in which he was involved in the chase and sinking of the *Bismarck*; he also participated in the D-Day assault in 1944. After the war, Golding returned to Bishop Wordsworth's school where he would teach for the next 16 years. In 1954, *Lord of the Flies* was published by Faber and Faber after being rejected by twenty-one other publishers. Because the book was an immediate success in England and an eventual best-seller in the United States, Golding was able to retire from teaching in order to pursue his writing career full time. *The Inheritors*, a tale of savagery about the extermination of the Neanderthals by the Homo Sapiens in prehistoric times, was published in 1955. Many critics deemed the novel superior to *Lord of the*

Flies. Shortly after its publication Golding became a fellow of the Royal Society of Literature. In 1956, *Pincher Martin* was published and subsequently republished in the United States as *The Two Lives of Christopher Martin*. Golding's play, *The Brass Butterfly*, was performed at Oxford and in London in 1958, and *Free Fall* was published in 1959. Golding's novels of the 1950s established him as one of the leading voices in British fiction.

Between 1960 and 1962, Golding becomes a frequent contributor of essays and book reviews to the *Spectator*. In 1960, he completed his master of arts degree at Brasenose College, and Golding spent the following year as writer in residence at Hollins College, Virginia, and toured as a lecturer at other American colleges. In 1963, *Lord of the Flies* was made into a film, and *The Spire* was published in 1964. A collection of essays, *The Hot Gates*, was published in 1965, and Golding was made a commander of the British Empire (CBE). In 1966, he became an honorary fellow of Brasenose College, Oxford, and the following year *The Pyramid*, a collection of novellas, was published. Golding was awarded an honorary doctorate of letters by Sussex University in 1970, and *The Scorpion God: Three Short Novels* was published the year after.

After a period of eight years in which no new work would be published by Golding, he experienced a critical resurgence with the publication of *Darkness Visible* in 1979, *Rites of Passage* in 1980, which won the Booker Prize for fiction, and a second collection of essays, *A Moving Target*, in 1982. In 1983, Golding reached the pinnacle of his career, receiving the Nobel Prize for Literature.

Golding continued to produce new works throughout the 1980s, publishing *The Paper Men* (1984), *An Egyptian Journal* (1985), *Close Quarters* (1987), the second volume of the sea trilogy begun with *Rites of Passage*, and *Fire down Below* (1989), the conclusion of the trilogy. In 1990, a new film version of *Lord of the Flies* was produced. William Golding died on June 19, 1993, at Perranarworthal. A draft of his novel *The Double Tongue*, left at the time of his death, was published posthumously in 1995.

The Story Behind the Story

Although William Golding initially planned to become a poet, that goal changed after the publication in 1954 of his first novel, *Lord of the Flies*. Considered by some to be his greatest work, it unquestionably is the novel that brought him the most attention. Read in many classrooms, the novel also has twice been made into a movie, and Golding received many letters about his book—from teachers, students, parents, psychiatrists, psychologists, and clergy, for example. Its accessibility and disturbing but vital message attracted readers in the aftermath of World War II and has continued to do so for decades later, when to many the world still appears a place of brutality and instability. The response to the work inspired Golding to give up poetry and stay with novel writing; while his first published book had been a collection of poems, he later said he did not even own a copy of it.

Golding fought in World War II, and when the war was over, he saw that people were still shocked about how Hitler and his regime inflicted such large-scale inhumane horrors on the Jews and others. Golding felt compelled to write about the human capacity for evil. But beyond this, he wanted to make it clear in his book that such behavior could occur anywhere, even in a seemingly advanced nation such as England. "The overall picture," Golding wrote about *Lord of the Flies*, "was to be the tragic lesson that the English have had to learn over a period of one hundred years; that one lot of people is inherently like any other lot of people; and that the only enemy of man is inside him." Golding wrote that the concept was really not new but people desperately needed to be reminded of it.

Golding also wrote about another concept he included in *Lord of the Flies*, what he called "off-campus history." Off-campus history, he explained, is different from academic history, which is taught in schools. It is a deep resentment handed down from generation to generation about a certain group or groups of people. He provided the example of a French woman who saw her country conquered in 1870, 1914, and 1940 and as a result had developed such an intense hatred for Germans that she shook whenever she thought of them. In Golding's novel, the parachutist, which some readers saw as a symbol that God is dead, was meant to stand for off-campus history, "the thing which threatens every child everywhere, the history of blood and intolerance, of ignorance and prejudice, the thing which is dead but won't lie down."

Due to the popularity of *Lord of the Flies*, Golding also described his other motivations in writing it and the decisions he made about the content and story. For example, having been one of a mass of English schoolboys who read Robert Ballantyne's idealized island adventure book *Coral Island*, Golding explained that he wanted to write a realistic alternative to it. In the Ballantyne book, as the critic James Baker has written, "everything comes off in exemplary style." The boys master their island environment, they use "sheer moral force" to easily defeat pirates, and use Christianity to readily convert and reform the cannibal inhabitants. Published in 1858, *Coral Island* maintained great popularity, and Golding incorporated a number of its characteristics into his novel in order to satirize it and other books like it. Golding even had characters in *Lord of the Flies* specifically refer to *Coral Island*. Early in Golding's book, when the characters are still excited about being on the beautiful island, they mention *Coral Island*, hopeful that they can mimic its atmosphere. Also, at the end of *Lord of the Flies*, the officer who rescues the boys is shocked that English boys could behave so poorly. When Ralph tries to explain that in the beginning things were running smoothly, the officer helps him out by saying it was like Coral Island. The contrast between what happened on Coral Island and what occurs in *Lord of the Flies* is severe. While the contrast between how life is at the beginning of *Lord of the Flies* and how it is at the end is also striking, it is even more disturbing, since the same boys act so very differently in a relatively short period of time. Not only do they kill other boys, but their desire to kill leads them to set such a destructive fire on the island that they destroy even their own source of protection and food; destruction seems to know no limits.

In regard to the ending of *Lord of the Flies*, Golding has explained that at the time he wrote the novel he believed that saving the character of Ralph was the only way to provide the opportunity for him to become self-aware (although his awareness provokes despair). This mix of hope and despair seems fitting for Golding, who in a 1964 interview observed, "I think that democratic attitude of voluntary curbs put on one's own nature is the only possible way for humanity, but I wouldn't like to say that it's going to work out, or survive."

List of Characters

Ralph is twelve years old, fair-haired, and attractive. Although he is readily elected chief, he still needs the help of Piggy's intelligence. His actions in the position are what prompt the reader to believe there is hope that practicality and civility can exist, even among youngsters left to care for themselves in the wild. His mistreatment of Piggy and his joining in the violence against Simon show how easily it is for even the good to succumb to evil.

Piggy is intelligent and sensitive, yet because of other, mostly physical characteristics, he is ultimately overpowered. He was raised by his aunt, is overweight, has asthma, cannot swim, and is the only boy who wears glasses. As intelligent as he is, he misjudges the evil of the others, believing they can be spoken with rationally and never realizing the seriousness of the situation and the potential for a deadly response. He stands as the example of the power of intelligence, strong enough to overcome many flaws but not strong enough to overcome a blind spot when it comes to understanding human nature.

Jack Merridew is the only boy who, early in the book, says he wants to be called by his last name. (In fact, only his and one other boy's last names are given.) He has red hair, an unpleasant face, and demands control over the choirboys he is placed in charge of in school. He is quick to show that he carries a large knife and almost never backs down from confrontation. He is excited about having an "army" of hunters and about having rules, because he anticipates the pleasure of punishing those who will break them. Ironically, he is the rule breaker who splits from the group, forces others to join him, and becomes more and more evil. He shows how easily evil gains power.

Simon, a member of the choir, is sensitive, quiet, and prone to fainting. He wishes he could speak publicly to the boys and be accepted by Ralph and his group, who for the most part find him "batty." He needs time to be alone, is brave and giving, and understands humanity. Golding has called him the Christ figure of the book, since he has a message to impart to the boys and becomes a martyr.

Sam and **Eric** are twins who function as if they are indistinguishable from each other. As a result, often they are referred to as "Samneric." They know each other's thoughts, complete each other's sentences, and are always together. Early on, they appear somewhat irresponsible when they abandon their key post at the fire and childish when they make fun of Ralph. Yet later in the book, they are loyal to him and want to do what is right.

Roger is another choir member who is brave enough to climb the mountain with Jack and Ralph to search for the beast. His mischief against the younger boys in the book's beginning is just a precursor to the danger he inflicts by throwing stones and then launching the largest rock of all as a weapon. Unlike many of the others, he does not need Jack to summon his evil side.

Maurice, Bill, and **Robert,** are the other older boys from the choir who join Jack's group. Initially, like the other choir members, they are imposing for the black robes and caps they wear. Ironically, the choir members are the only ones described as wearing crosses and yet are the first to join Jack's evil "tribe" (except for Simon). Later, they don the "savage" war paint, hunt, and follow Jack's orders. They are mentioned by name only a few times and are not given distinct personalities, except perhaps for Maurice, who a few times shows he understands how to defuse a tense situation but also seemingly foolishly increases the fear in the little ones because of his comments at a meeting. These boys are an example of the danger of followers.

The **"littluns"** (short for "little ones") are the youngest of the boys, each being roughly six years old. They are not differentiated as individuals. They can be playful but are plagued with fearful fantasies and nightmares. Since they are so young, they can contribute little and to some degree must be taken care of.

Percival Wemys Madison is a littlun who is prone to crying and who prompts other of the youngest boys to do so as well. When asked for his name, he gives his full name and address, but only part of his phone number. Now unable to remember what his parents must have carefully trained him in and emphasized as important, he is another symbol of the breakdown of civilization on the island. When he says the beast comes from the sea, he inspires chaos at a meeting, indicating the ease with which fear overtakes most of the group.

The **boy with the wine-colored scar** is a littlun who first makes public his and the other young children's fears of a beast. He becomes a symbol of what happens when accountability is not practiced by those who should be responsible.

Summary and Analysis

At the beginning of *Lord of the Flies*, we read of a fair-haired boy who is dragging his school sweater and sweating as he attempts to make his way over rocks and through a rough hot jungle toward a lagoon. A voice calls to this boy to wait, which he does as he pulls up his "stockings with an automatic gesture that made the jungle seem for a moment like the Home Counties," the group of counties nearest London. Out of the undergrowth appears another boy, who is shorter than the first, very fat, and wearing thick eyeglasses and a "greasy wind-breaker," despite the heat.

The squat boy asks for the man with the megaphone, but he is told that there is no such man and that they are on an island; it seems that there may be no adults on the island at all. The possibility is disturbing to the younger boy, but the older one finds it so delightful that he stands on his head, grinning for a moment. The younger boy is unfazed by the other and continues to ponder the situation. The reader, like these boys, must piece together what has happened. Through the boys' dialogue, alternately overly optimistic and realistic, we learn that these boys and others were in a plane crash. The nose of the plane went down in flames, but the cabin crashed through the jungle trees, landing near enough to the water to be pulled out to sea, perhaps with some boys still aboard.

The smaller boy asks the other what his name is, and the taller boy says his name is Ralph, but does not ask the smaller boy for his name in return. Ralph starts again toward the lagoon, now going faster, slowing only because he trips. The smaller boy's breathing is more strained from trying to keep up, and he tells Ralph that his aunt has told him not to run since he has asthma. Ralph makes fun of the boy's improper pronunciation, but we realize he speaks ungrammatically as well.

While Ralph is described as standing among "skull-like coconuts," he remains enthralled with the freedom of the island, joyfully removes all of his clothes, and is nearly entranced by the beach and water that they have reached. The narrator now tells us that Ralph is twelve, and while he has the physique of a boxer he does not have the "devil" in him. Again he stands on his head in delight as the other young boy ponders their situation; the younger one says that they will have to learn all the others' names (another hint to Ralph that he still does not know this boy's name) and that they should have a meeting. Finally he tells Ralph that he just does not want anyone to call him the nickname assigned to him at school, which, he whispers, was "Piggy." At this, Ralph laughs wildly, dances, and pretends he is a fighter plane attacking Piggy. Piggy takes some pleasure in the attention but repeats that Ralph cannot tell the others.

The two boys explore a little farther and find a raised jetty, with shade and an enchanting beach pool with warm water, glittering fish, and coral. Ralph plunges in with delight, and Piggy sticks one toe in tentatively. Ralph continues to stand out as the more fortunate boy. He learned to swim, whereas Piggy could not because of his asthma; Ralph's dad is a commander in the navy, whereas Piggy's dad is dead and his mother was not around to raise him.

While Piggy's weaknesses seem almost in excess, he is quite intelligent and practical. When Ralph boyishly boasts that his father will come and rescue them, Piggy asks how he will find them, and Ralph scavenges for an answer that Piggy reminds him is impossible. Ralph's dad would not be told by the people at the airport where the boys are, Piggy says. He questions Ralph: "Didn't you hear what the pilot said? About the atom bomb? They're all dead." This, finally, is enough to bring Ralph out of his idyllic daydreaming, and he pulls himself out of the warm water and ponders the situation. Piggy persists in making it clear that no one knows where the boys are, meaning they may stay there until they die. The heat seems to greatly intensify, and Ralph again shows his return to reality by getting dressed.

Piggy insists that they find the others and "do something," but Ralph has already returned to his dreaming. He spies a conch shell in the water, and as Piggy expounds on its value, Ralph manuevers to get it. When Piggy warns him to be careful, Ralph "absently" tells him to "shut up," pointing to the contrast between each boy's level of concern for the other. Curiously, though, as much as Ralph feels that Piggy is interrupting his bliss, Piggy's intently sticking by Ralph's side makes sense. Although Ralph is the one that sees the shell and determines a way to reach it, he still needs Piggy's help.

Piggy realizes that by blowing into the shell they can alert the others, indicating the significance of the chapter's title, "The Sound of the Shell." Piggy knows the technique for getting the shell to sound, but Ralph blows into it since Piggy has asthma. It takes a few tries on Ralph's part, but then the shell's "deep, harsh note boomed" and grew into "a strident blare," scattering birds and other wild animals and achieving the goal of alerting the others. A boy of about six is the first to appear; Piggy helps him to the platform and asks him his name, as Ralph continues sounding the shell. While the shell, with its white appearance, has seemed only a positive image, Ralph's "face was dark with the violent pleasure" of making it bellow, indicating not necessarily that the shell itself is symbolically evil but that Ralph potentially has a dark side.

Piggy greets each child that appears and tries to memorize each one's name. They sit on the fallen tree trunks expectantly and are described as giving Piggy "the same simple obedience that they had given to the men with megaphones." This is the second vague reference to the power of the men with megaphones, but now that we know there has been an atomic blast we theorize that the men may have been responsible for evacuating the children before the attacks began. Aside from the first boy's name, Johnny, the only other names mentioned are those of the twins who appear, Sam and Eric, who also have light hair like Ralph. They are energetic, grinning, and nearly identical, and when Piggy tries to get their names straight but makes a mistake, the whole group laughs.

Yet there is an unusual black "creature" also approaching the platform, which Ralph is the first to spot. As it gets closer, the boys see that it is actually a group of boys dressed in eccentric black cloaks and caps, each cap having a silver badge. They are marching in twos behind "[t]he boy who controlled them," who is also dressed in this odd way but has a golden badge on his cap. He is tall and thin, yet has red hair and a "crumpled" face that is "ugly without silliness." His eyes are described as "turning, or ready to turn, to anger," and he is the first of his group to approach the gathered boys, making his cloaked companions, who we find out are choir members, wait several yards back. One boy faints, we assume from the heat, but are then told that this is commonplace for him.

Piggy is intimidated and moves to Ralph's side farthest away from this group and nervously wipes his glasses. The choir boys refer to their leader as Merridew, and he asks those gathered whether there are grown-ups on the island. They explain that there are none present and that they have called a meeting to get everyone's name and decide what to do next. Merridew scoffs at the collecting of first names, calling it childish and insisting he be called by his last name; throughout the rest of the book, though, he is called Jack. He tells Piggy he is talking too much, adding, "Shut up, Fatty" and provoking laughter from the others. Unfortunately the laughter only increases when Ralph tells the group Piggy's name.

The decision is made to appoint Ralph chief, since he is tall, attractive, and has possession of the delicate yet powerful conch shell; he is described as having "a stillness" about him. To be fair, Ralph asks for those who would rather have Jack as chief to raise their hands; only the choir does, with "dreary obedience." Curiously, Piggy shows the same lack of enthusiasm when he and all the others raise their hands in support of Ralph.

The new chief decides that the first order of business is to determine if, in fact, they are on an island. Ralph says that he, Jack, and Simon, the boy who fainted, will explore, while everyone else remains behind. Jack draws some attention when he shows his large knife. Piggy wants to go but is turned away.

The three boys set off, happy and laughing excitedly, and Ralph again joyfully stands on his head. After walking to the end of the island, Ralph decides it is best to climb the mountain. The boys notice tracks that Jack says are from animals. Ralph, curious about them, "peered into the darkness under the trees. The forest minutely vibrated." It is an ominous description, yet the author tells us just this and nothing of the boys' reactions.

As they get to the toughest part of their climb, they are awed to be exploring where perhaps no one else has ever been. Since in this terrain Ralph cannot stand on his head, his usual exuberant action, he instead starts a playful scuffle with the others. The action seems innocuous enough and certainly boyish, yet at the same time it is also an indication of trouble to come.

As the three near the top of the rocky incline, Jack notices a huge, loose rock. He calls for the others to help him push, and the rock is eventually dislodged, smashing into the forest below, which shakes "as with the passage of an enraged monster." It is a destructive move, but the boys only see it as great fun and revel in their triumph.

Finally at the top, they see butterflies and a lavish hanging blue flower that spreads down into the forest canopy. The boys find that they were right in their assumption that they are on an island, and Ralph announces that it all belongs to them. They note the island's rough boatlike shape, its coral reef, the gash where their plane landed, and the platform where they have left the other boys, who now seem to be mere insects.

Again, they feel triumphant. They see no signs of other humans, and Jack is excited about finding food and hunting and catching "things" they will need to survive until they are rescued. Hearing this, the boys realize they are hungry and begin scrambling down the rocks, stopping near the edge of the forest when they come across a piglet trapped in the tangled growth. Jack slashes a flower with his knife, before raising it again above the small struggling creature. When he hesitates, however, they realize the "enormity" of killing, and the animal gets away. Jack is white and provides excuses for why he did not stab the pig. He promises that next time will be different and sticks his knife into a tree trunk.

The three boys return to the others in **chapter 2**. It is afternoon, and they reassemble when they hear Ralph blow the conch. Golding's interplay of light and dark is evident here as the older boys, who were not part of the choir, stand to the right of Ralph illuminated by the sun. The former choirboys, who have discarded their robes, stand to the left of Ralph in the dark. Ralph is somewhat uncomfortable in his chief role and gets no help from Piggy, but when he starts to speak he immediately realizes the words flow freely and clearly.

Ralph reveals their discoveries: They are on an island that appears to be uninhabited. Jack interrupts to say an "army" is needed for hunting. Then all three boys speak of the trapped pig they saw, and Jack again stabs a tree his knife, vowing to kill the next pig they see.

Ralph then announces that, as in school, if someone wants to speak he must raise his hand. Ralph will then give the boy the conch shell, and he alone will speak without interruption from anyone but Ralph. At the very moment that he is explaining how they will avoid interruptions, Jack interrupts, jubilant, with thoughts of punishing those who break the new rules.

Piggy takes the shell and says Ralph has more to say, something that is important. Like an expert orator, Ralph pauses to increase their interest and tells them that no one knows where they are, since they never arrived at their final destination. Their plane was shot down before they arrived, and they may not be rescued for a long time. The group is silent, and then Ralph grins and explains the positive aspects of their situation; it is like being in a book, he says, and they all become excited.

A small boy about six years old is pushed out from the group sitting in front of Ralph so that he can speak. Only after being prodded does he come forward, and still Piggy must lean over and listen to him and then do the talking for him. The boy wants to know what they plan to do about the very large "snake-thing" that he saw in the woods, what he calls a "beastie." With this, the platform becomes cooler, either from the setting sun or from the varied breezes. The boys are disturbed.

Ralph explains that there is no such thing as the wild beast, but the little boy persists in his story and the others are grave, calmed only when Jack says that if there is such a thing they will hunt it down and kill it. Ralph grows increasingly annoyed and frustrated, suggesting that such a creature is an impossibility, and the group falls grimly silent. He shifts to speaking about the positive—they will be saved, since the queen has a map of every island in the world. All are relieved and applaud loudly, leaving Ralph feeling triumphant.

He tells them that to be saved they must make a fire on top of the mountain, and at once they get up, with Jack joining in and calling for them to follow him. (The chapter's name is "Fire on the Mountain.") Ralph and Piggy are left, with Piggy perturbed by the others acting "like a crowd of kids!" This is one of the earliest indications that he does not understand human nature. He is surprised when Ralph rushes off after the boys, but then he, too, follows with the conch.

All but Piggy scavenge for materials to fuel the fire, only to realize that they do not know how to start a fire without matches. Jack says they can use Piggy's glasses and snatches them. The fire roars quickly, and the boys race for more wood, but it seems impossible to keep it burning, and the fire dies. Ralph says that the fire was no good anyway, since it was all flame and no smoke, which is what will get the attention of a passing ship. Piggy, still with the conch, chimes in, but Jack cuts him off. Piggy keeps trying to speak, but then Ralph takes the shell, saying they must appoint groups to look after the fire.

Jack takes the shell and gives his hearty endorsement, again advocating rules: "After all, we're not savages. We're English, and the English are best at everything. So we've got to do the right things." He says that the choir, his hunters, will take responsibility for the fire and keep a lookout.

Piggy takes the shell, still trying to be heard, but then stops when he looks "down the unfriendly side of the mountain," since the fire is spreading there rapidly. The boys cheer as they watch it take over, and Ralph recognizes that they have grown silent out of awe at the power they have unleashed. "The knowledge and the awe," Golding writes, "made him [Ralph] savage." Ralph orders Piggy to shut up. Piggy is hurt but defends his right to speak since he has the conch. All are still intent on the fire as Piggy tries to get their attention then calls to Ralph, who is also entranced by "the splendid, awful sight." Piggy chastises them for not acting properly, warning that this will keep them from being rescued. He also says the little kids were never all counted, since they had run amok when Ralph, Jack, and Simon left and Piggy was supposed to have taken their names.

Ralph is angry, but the situation becomes even worse when Piggy says that some of the "littluns" are in the area where the fire has now spread to. He gasps for breath as he says that he does not see the little boy who had been so worried about the snakes. He is interrupted yet again, this time by a tree exploding in flames, provoking the little boys to scream as they see the creepers move into view. Piggy falls, gasping, asking again where the little boy is, and the fire continues.

Chapter 3 takes place some time later, since we are told that Jack's hair is now noticeably longer and that some meetings have taken place. The chapter opens with Jack hunting by himself, bent down, "dog-like," with a long spear and wearing only tattered shorts. Compelled to kill, Jack seems a practiced hunter yet he is frustrated with his lack of success; his eyes "seem bolting and nearly mad." He throws his spear yet misses a pig, and after a day of hunting, sweaty from the oppressive heat, he rejoins the rest of the boys.

At this point, frustration is consuming Ralph as well. Jack sees him attempting to create shelters with Simon. Two shaky ones have been erected, but a third has just fallen. Ralph, like Jack, has to stop his task, and when he sees Jack, he complains that the twice-a-day meetings do not seem to be working, that rather than helping with the shelters the boys only work for five minutes and go off to play, swim, eat, or go hunting. Jack is quick to remind him that they want meat, but Ralph says they need shelters, that the hunters left hours ago and that they have not caught anything yet anyway. There is a hint of madness in Jack's eyes as he tries to explain his compulsion to kill, but Ralph is insistent about the shelters, and both boys become angry.

Ralph turns away and changes the subject, explaining that there is another reason that the shelters are important. He looks into Jack's "fierce, dirty face" and tells him that the youngest boys (who they now regularly call the "littluns") as well as some of the older boys are thoroughly frightened and talk and scream as they dream at night. Simon breaks in and says it appears the boys no longer realize that this is a "good island," as if they truly believe in the "beastie," which no one has mentioned since the first little boy did (who we assume was killed in the fire). Ralph echoes Simon's words about the island being a good one, but Jack, the one intent on killing and less aware of the others' needs, does not. The two boys grin as they recall the "glamour" of their first day exploring on the island.

Even so, Ralph says they need the shelters, and Jack shows he is in agreement by finishing Ralph's sentence: they need the shelters as a kind of home. The shelters are of central importance to Golding as well, since the chapter is titled, "Huts on the Beach."

Curiously, though, Jack is not as fearless as he appears. He explains that when he is hunting by himself "you can feel as if you're not hunting, but—being hunted, as if something's behind you all the time in the jungle. . . . That's how you can feel in the forest. Of course there's nothing in it. Only—only—." Ralph is incredulous but controls his reaction.

Meanwhile, Simon, whom Ralph has just described to Jack as odd, has gone off by himself. He is amid the acres of fruit trees, plentiful with fruit, flowers, and bees. He helps the littluns who follow him get the best fruit they cannot reach and continues to do so until all are satisfied. Again he goes off by himself to a small hidden spot in the jungle and stays there as evening approaches. The white flowers he had been intrigued by and described as candlelike on their first day on the island, while the others had seen no use for them, open in the starlight, with their aroma encompassing the entire island.

Chapter 4 continues with a description of nature. The morning is good on the island, but, we are told, "Strange things happened at midday." Mirages appear on the horizon as if a bump on the land. They disappear at the end of the afternoon, which brings cooler temperatures but also signals the menacing approach of darkness, which prompts fear in many of the boys.

The "littluns," each roughly six years old, live separately from the older boys. They have built sandcastles along the little river. One day, three of the littluns are playing when they are interrupted by two of the bigger boys, Roger and Maurice, who destroy the castles on the way to the beach. Even though no adults are present to scold them, Maurice feels a twinge of guilt for causing the destruction, whereas Roger seems not to and is described as someone who initially seemed unsociable but now appears "forbidding."

Roger is not content with the small interference he has caused. Rather than jumping into the water for his swim, he follows the biggest of the three boys, Henry, that had been playing and proceeds to tease him. Henry has moved away from the other two young boys, fascinated by the tiny creatures, scavengers, washed in with the waves. Yet even this is a disturbing pastime, for Henry is making small ruts and paths in the sand and is thrilled to be controlling the creatures' movements by doing so, excited by the "illusion of mastery."

Roger throws stones at the involved Henry but deliberately misses, still abiding by the rules of his old life, even though, Golding writes, it is "a civilization that knew nothing of him and was in ruins." While there is some hope that civility is still possible, since even the most threatening of the boys is not willing to cause too much harm, the question arises as to whether the boys will still react the same way when they find out that most of the outside world is ruined, or whether they will react the same way after being on the island for a longer time.

Roger is called away by Jack, who has found something that should help in their hunting. With Jack are three other older boys, the twins Sam and Eric, and Bill. Jack takes colored clay that he has found and paints his face, explaining that this will make it harder for the pigs to detect him in the brush. Jack is thrilled with his face painting, and as he dances his laughter transforms into "bloodthirsty snarling." The camouflage hides the true Jack, now "liberated from shame and self-consciousness." The face repulses Bill to the point that he laughs, grows quiet, and then leaves, but the face compels the twins, after some protest, to follow Jack to meet with the others who are preparing to surround a pig. It is unclear whether Roger goes with them.

While only one boy has painted his face with the stark colors so far, almost all of the others are frequently described as pushing their long hair back from their foreheads. The unkempt hair makes them appear less civilized, but beyond this its growth is something out of their control, suggesting the notion that becoming less civilized is out of their control as well. Additionally, their hair hangs in their eyes, presumably making them increasingly blind. It is something that afflicts all of them except Piggy, whose hair remains wispy and never seems to grow.

We return to Ralph, who is unaware of what's going on with the older boys; he is just out of the bathing pool and followed by Piggy. To Ralph, Piggy is boring and fat, but there is pleasure to be derived from teasing him. When Piggy sees Ralph smile at this thought he is happy for what he believes is a sign of friendliness, especially since he is usually seen as an outsider because of his weight, eyeglasses, asthma, lack of assisting with manual labor, and accent, the last of which "did not matter," Golding tells us. The reader has been made privy to the various abuses Piggy has so far suffered, yet Golding now asserts that Piggy's accent, specifically, did not matter. At least one critic disagrees with Golding and has commented that the accent, in fact, is chiefly at the root of Piggy's mistreatment, as it is a trait frequently seen as differentiating classes and indicating status. Piggy's faults and physical characteristics, on the other hand, could be present in an individual of any background.

What seems an average moment on the beach turns serious when Ralph jumps up and announces that he sees smoke far out at sea. All the other boys run to the water's edge to look, while Piggy observes at the top of the mountain and asks if they, in fact, are producing any smoke signal. Ralph again is revealed to be the one who has to do the work; not only has he spotted the ship at sea but when the others are doubtful about the status of their own smoke signal, he is the first to start scrambling up the mountain. When he is partially up, cursing along the way, Ralph realizes they will need Piggy's glasses if the fire is out, but Piggy is far behind. Ralph presses on despite this, and after reaching the top, finds that the fire is out and those responsible for it are gone. He screams insanely and repeatedly for the ship to come back.

Bitterly angry, Ralph spots Jack and some of the others approaching them, including the twins, who, we learn, were supposed to have been tending fire but are now carrying the carcass of a pig on a stake. The scantily dressed boys, some in black caps, are chanting, and only as they get closer can Ralph and the others make it out: "Kill the pig. Cut her throat. Spill her blood."

Jack reaches the mountaintop first. He and all the others are excited to tell how they cornered and killed the pig. When Ralph tells them they let the fire go out, Jack sees the comment as irrelevant and continues relating what happened. Although the killing is ultimately described as "a long satisfying drink," Jack, beneath his laughter, still shows some twinges of repulsion, even as he laughs,

Curiously, it is Ralph's voice that is described as "savage," since Ralph has been pushed to his limit by the hunters' irresponsibility. He loudly tells them that they had seen a ship, which finally silences the hunters. Jack tries to evade responsibility. When Ralph continues to press him and Piggy joins in, Jack says he needed as many people as he could gather for the hunt, and once again the argument turns to the tasks of obtaining meat versus building shelters. Jack pushes his hair down on his forehead, exactly the opposite of Ralph, who had earlier been pushing his back. The long, overgrown hair emphasizes his bestial qualities even further when, tousling his hair, he unwittingly spreads blood from the hunted pig on his forehead.

When Piggy starts to chastise Jack again, some of the other hunters join in. Jack lashes out, punching Piggy in the stomach, and even after Ralph steps forward Jack smacks Piggy again, this time in the head, knocking his glasses off. Simon rescues them, but now one side of his glasses is broken, putting Piggy at even more of a disadvantage. Yet Piggy is not intimidated and threatens Jack, only to have Jack mimic him. This provokes the others to laugh, and even Ralph almost joins in but he is angry instead at his own weakness.

Ralph rebukes Jack again, and Jack finally apologizes, not for his treatment of Piggy but for letting the fire go out. He is so clearly established as a leader that Sam and Eric, who had also been assigned responsibility for the fire, never appear guilty, as if Jack has such control over them that they had no choice but to join him in the hunt. The hunters admire Jack for apologizing and wait to hear Ralph graciously accept, but he cannot. Instead Ralph tells them to light the fire, and all join in, relieved to have put the squabble behind them.

The roasted pig brings the group together, even Ralph and Piggy to some extent. When Ralph is given a piece of meat, he is described as chewing on it like a wolf, even though he would have liked to have turned it down. Even within the chief, the line dividing civilization and barbarity has become increasingly blurred. Jack makes a point of not giving any meat to Piggy, who asks disoriently where his is and gets an angry reply from Jack. Ralph feels uneasy but remains still and silent. Simon gives Piggy his meat, only to be laughed at by the twins, causing him to hang his head in shame. Jack grows increasingly angry and can only blurt out short phrases. They all fall silent until Maurice asks about the hunt.

The hunters describe their experience and inspire the grinning twins to mimic the noises of the dying boar. Maurice then pretends to be the pig, and the hunters encircle him and pretend to beat him, dance, and intone their ritualized pig chant. Ralph is described as "envious and resentful," and when the boys stop their revelry, he says they will have an assembly at the platform immediately and leaves.

Chapter 5 opens with Ralph preparing for the meeting. While there have been several meetings already, this is the first time that Ralph spends any time preparing. He chooses to walk on the beach to think because it is the only place where he can walk freely without having to watch where he is going. Ralph comes to realize how exhausted he is by life on the island and recalls the first day when he explored with Simon and Jack, remembering it as if "it were part of a brighter childhood." There is a hopelessness and sadness in the comparison, for Ralph is still young but feels distanced from his own childhood; whether he will be happy in the future seems unknown.

Ralph also realizes how "unpleasant" it is to be wearing a dirty shirt, uncomfortable shorts, and to have hair hanging in his eyes. As he approaches the platform, he sees how its triangular shape is not quite right and that the tipping log where many of the boys sit has never been fixed. His "strange mood of speculation that was so foreign to him" continues as he prepares to sound the conch shell. He realizes that a chief must be wise and a good thinker but recognizes that he is not a strong or shrewd thinker, especially in comparison to Piggy. His values have shifted.

When all the boys have gathered, Ralph tries to explain things simply, so that even the smallest will understand. He states that the assembly was called to discuss a serious matter, to set things straight, and proceeds to describe what they are doing wrong, namely that decisions they make in meetings that then are not carried out. They had decided, for example, to collect freshwater and to keep it in a certain place, to use one section of the rocks as a lavatory, yet these rules were only followed for a short while. Similarly, while many pitched in to build the first shelter, by the time they got to building the fourth, only Simon and Ralph completed the work.

As he speaks, Ralph is strong and steady, although at times the listening boys are giggling and not recognizing the seriousness of the situation. Ralph adds that without the fire they will die, but even this does not seem to focus the group's attention. He also announces that from then on they will only have a fire on the mountain. Many want to speak against this decision, but Ralph talks over the group and again tells them that they must listen to him since they named him chief.

Jack wants to interrupt, but Ralph says he still has more to say and then tells the group what they can talk about. He says that things started to go wrong when the boys began to get frightened, and he tells them they can work on "kind of deciding on the fear." He tells them again that there is nothing to fear. But Jack assumes a different approach. He is angry and calls the young boys names for being babies. He differentiates, too, between fear and the beast in the forest that many still believe is there. He says he has walked the entire island and no beast exists, so they should not think about it any longer. "And as for the fear—," he adds, "you'll have to put up with that like the rest of us." But there is no beast, he tells them again, which draws applause from the group.

Piggy speaks next, and even though he is made fun of, he persists and explains that not only is there no beast but there is no reason to be frightened. He purports that the world is scientific and that soon men will be traveling to Mars. He repeats that there is nothing to fear but then pauses and adds, "Unless we get frightened of people." When the others laugh and poke fun at this statement, Piggy turns to let the "littluns" speak, so, he says, the older boys can show them how silly they are. But when the first one speaks and describes his terrifying experience, even though Ralph explains that the boy was having a nightmare at the time, the group sympathizes and is unsettled.

Piggy draws another small boy forward, his behavior similar to that of the boy who initially spoke about the beast when they boys first arrived on the island and then ended up lost and dying in the fire. At first, the boy will not speak, and Ralph and the others force him to do so. He provides his whole name, as well as his address and the beginning of his telephone number before he starts weeping. The others tell him to be quiet, but he cannot stop. When other small boys start crying as well, the only thing that finally quiets them is Maurice performing some funny stunts.

Again the older boys dismiss the idea of the beast and press this small boy, Percival, to explain where this beast could possibly be hiding. He replies that it comes out of the sea, causing a new wave of fear among the group and explaining the chapter's title, "Beast from Water." Maurice becomes the first older boy to admit they do not know for sure that the beast does not exist, a confession that provokes complete chaos. Amid shouts and yelling, Simon then asserts that the beast may only be "us." Simon tries vainly to explain "mankind's essential illness," after which a member of the group suggests that maybe Simon is really speaking of a kind of ghost. In reaction to this assertion, both Piggy and Jack want to speak and end up fighting for the conch shell, until Ralph interjects.

Ralph admits that he made a mistake in having the meeting so late, that perhaps the topic is not an appropriate one to be discussed as it gets darker. While earlier he had shown growth by realizing Piggy's intellectual abilities, at this meeting he appears to have diminished in his role as leader. While he recognized the need for the meeting and started it off on a strong note, the topic of the beast was one that had been discussed previously and had not been effectively resolved then. Bringing up the beast again shows Ralph's seemingly irrational belief in the power of common sense to always triumph. To make matters worse, he asks for a vote to show if they believe in ghosts, even though, again, he probably will be unable to dissuade any believers.

In an attempt to save Ralph and the situation, Piggy berates the group: "What are we? Humans? Or animals? Or savages? What's grownups going to think? Going off—hunting pigs—letting fires out—and now!" Jack tells Piggy to shut up, and when Ralph finally and without prodding stands up for Piggy, Jack loses control. He orders Ralph to be silent as well and questions why he should be chief, since he gives orders that do not make sense, cannot hunt or sing, and always favors Piggy. Ralph shouts back that Jack is breaking the rules, "the only thing we've got!" Jack, however, says he does not care about the rules, gives a wild scream, and jumps off the platform. The participants disperse, screaming and laughing, and then chant in a revolving dancing mass.

Piggy and Ralph remain on the platform. Piggy urges him to sound the conch, but Ralph says if he does and the others do not come they will have lost everything—the fire will not be tended and there will be no rescue. "We'll be like animals," he says. Ralph draws the shell to his lips but then lowers it. He asks Piggy if ghosts exist and says he should not be chief after all. Piggy tries to reassure him, when they realize that someone else is sitting with them as well, Simon, who also says Ralph must remain chief.

Piggy wonders what would happen to him if Ralph was not chief. Ralph, again unaware, says nothing would happen to him, but Piggy explains that Jack hates Ralph and Piggy, and since Jacl cannot fight Ralph, given the opportunity he will fight Piggy. Simon concurs. The boys voice their wishes that a parent or caretaker were present, as then everything would be all right. As much as Piggy and Simon are keen observers, they still hold childish views of adults, believing adults always know what to do and would never have devolved into disputes and lazy, irresponsible habits like the children on the island have. Ralph seemingly foolishly wishes that the adults could give them some sign. The three are now so disturbed that they reach for one another when they hear a chilling noise from the dark. The wail comes from Percival, although the three boys do not at first know what the sound is. Percival, the boy that no one wants to believe, is the last voice in the chapter, instilling fear among the strongest boys and deepening the pervasive sense of foreboding.

The beast, and the fear it provokes, reenters the narrative and will remain the focus of the next chapter, **chapter 6**, titled "Beast from Air." The boys settle Percival in a shelter before falling asleep themselves, all the while unaware of the battle being fought ten miles above their heads. Ironically, the boys get the sign Ralph had requested but fail to recognize it for what it is. Unnoticed by them, an explosion occurs overhead and from it drops a person dangling in a parachute. The parachute eventually gets caught among the rocks of the mountaintop. Hanging by the lines and blown by the wind, the man's body rocks back and forth depending on the gust.

The twins, Sam and Eric, are also unaware of what is occurring, once again responsible for the fire on the mountaintop but not doing their job, since they are both asleep and the fire is nearly out. When they wake up, they are relieved that they can get it started again and laugh at the thought of how angry Ralph would have been if he had seen what had happened. Only fifteen yards away from them is the tangled parachutist, whose parachute is making noise as it blows and flaps in the wind. When the two hear it and see a dark humped figure, the frightened brothers scramble down the mountain.

Ralph is having pleasant dreams, but the terrified twins interrupt his sleep. They tell him they saw the beast. Ralph calls to Piggy for the spears, but they dare not venture out at that time and wait until morning when they can hold another meeting. The twins describe the beast as furry, with wings, teeth, and claws and say that it followed them down the mountain, slinking behind the trees. All are horrified. Jack asks who is ready to hunt the creature, but Ralph hesitates, wondering what they can do with meager wooden spears, who will take care of the small boys if all the others leave, and how they can find a beast that leaves no tracks.

Ralph says Piggy will stay with the small boys; Jack contends that this is favoritism once again. Piggy is anxious about being left behind, and Jack berates him, characteristically angry once again. When Piggy says he has the conch and therefore the right to speak, Jack says the rules about speaking are unnecessary, that there are only a few people who should be speaking and making decisions. The battle continues when Ralph fumes and tells Jack to sit down, but Jack refuses to comply. He cannot wait to go, saying this is a hunter's job, but Ralph reminds him again that there are no tracks and that they also have to relight the fire that must have gone out by now. Now, the boys are on Ralph's side.

Ralph asks Jack what part of the island he has not yet patrolled and decides that is where they will go to search, at the tip where the large rocks are found. At Ralph's direction, the older boys eat first rather than just setting out, and Ralph decides that Jack can lead. Simon expresses to Ralph his doubts about the existence of the beast, although he does not share this view with the others. It makes no sense, he thinks, that a beast with claws would leave no tracks and would not be fast enough to catch the twins. Golding tells us, "However Simon thought of the beast, there rose before his inward sight the picture of a human at once heroic and sick." Here, Simon displays his ability, unique among the group at sensing or intuiting the truth. In this case, it makes sense that the parachutist was heroic and now is possibly sick or harmed. After contemplating his vision, Simon becomes perturbed at his inability to speak in front of the others. Then, as he slows down to walk next to Ralph and is pleased to see him smile at him, Simon runs into a tree he failed to notice, again a belittled and comic figure rather than one with an important message to impart.

When they arrive at the end of the island near the bottom of the rocky cliff, Ralph realizes he must go forward since he is the chief. As he hesitates and asks if this really is the logical place to go, Simon voices his disbelief that a beast exists, although none takes it seriously. Ralph makes it to the narrow neck of rock and looks to the other side of the island, unsettled to see the massive swell of the Pacific Ocean that "seemed like the breathing of some stupendous creature." This is the first clue the reader is given indicating the geographic location of the island, and we realize that the boys are indeed very far from home.

Jack then catches up to Ralph, not comfortable letting him go ahead on his own. They make it to the last peak, and Jack starts to ask Ralph if he remembers the first day when they had explored there, but his sentence trails off unfinished as he realizes all the negative things that have happened between them since. Jack looks at the huge rock and thinks of how great it would be to heave it down on an enemy. Ralph looks over in the direction of the mountain where the fire should be and is disturbed to see that once again it has gone out. He decides they should go climb the mountain, since the fire will need to be rekindled and that is where the twins saw the beast.

Ralph is intent on getting up the mountain, but when the others realize Ralph and Jack have found no trace of the beast, they start to play and roll rocks. As Ralph tries to convince the others to follow his plan, Golding interjects: "A strange thing happened in his [Ralph's] head. Something flittered there in front of his mind like a bat's wing, obscuring his idea." A vision, not yet fully formed or grasped by Ralph seems to be assembling in his mind. He tells the boys they are wasting their time when they need a fire, and the others argue with him and plead that he not press them immediately into this next mission. Angry, Ralph hits his knuckles against a rock as he has done before on this trip, but this time it does not seem to hurt. He, like Simon, stands out from the others. He berates the boys again, and they fall "mutinously" silent.

Chapter 7 directly continues the action of the preceding chapter, again indicating an urgency and adding to the tension the search for the beast has provoked. There is an ominous note to the chapter's title, "Shadows and Tall Trees," yet a relief in it as well, since, unlike the two previous chapter titles, this one does not include the word *beast*.

The boys are continuing along the rocks to get to the mountaintop. They stop to eat some fruit, and Ralph realizes how hot it is and how good it would be to wash his stiff shirt, cut his hair, bathe with soap, and brush his teeth. On this side of the island, flanked by the vast roaring sea instead of the calm lagoon, "one was helpless, one was condemned, one was—." Ralph does not finish his thought, but the brutishness of nature on this side of the island only reinforces the boys' fear and the erosion of their ragtag community. Ralph's thoughts are interrupted when Simon tells him that he will make it home. Ralph, more the pragmatist and also perhaps struck by the strength of Simon's assertion, asks him how he "knows" this. Simon is content to explain that he just thinks it, to which Ralph calls him "batty." Still, the two end up smiling at each other, apparently each accepting the other and perhaps thankful to be focusing, even for a moment, on a dream.

Roger sees signs of pigs, and Ralph agrees that they can hunt them, as long as doing so will take them in the right direction. So the tense group of hunters slowly advances, and when they have to stop for a moment, Ralph daydreams of his life at home. He, like Piggy, had a rough or challenging childhood back in England, since he had lived in several homes and his mother had not always been with the family; nonetheless, the daydream is idyllic just the same. The boy's flights of fancy and escapism contrast with the harsh surroundings and the tension of the hunt, making the reality of the boys' current situation appear even bleaker.

The daydream is interrupted when Ralph sees the others scrambling and then a boar charging directly toward him. He throws his sharpened stick, lodging it in the animal's snout. Jack orders the group in the chase, but the boar gets away.

Despite the overall defeat, Ralph feels victorious for having inflicted the wound. He is excited, asks the others to confirm that they saw it, and then "sunned himself in their new respect and felt that hunting was good after all." Jack is displeased that Ralph threw at the wrong time, and when he shows that he is bloody from the boar's tusks, attention shifts to him.

Ralph, not to be deterred, explains how he thrust at the boar, and Robert snarls at him, pretending to be the animal, as the others join in jabbing him. Jack, again in charge, tells them to encircle Robert, who is still pretending but then, in actual pain, calls out for them to stop. Jack holds him by the hair and is ready with his knife; the others join in their chant: "Kill the pig! Cut his throat! Kill the pig! Bash him in!" Ralph, too, is jabbing and fights to get closer. His "desire to squeeze and hurt was over-mastering," Golding writes.

When Jack signals, the boys stop, dreaming up what they can do next time to improve what Jack calls "the game." Robert, even though he has just been the victim, says they need a real pig, since they actually have to kill it. The suggestions end with Jack's idea that they could just use a "littlun." Everyone laughs, and this only increases the intensity of this chilling episode.

Ralph takes charge, saying they must move on. Maurice and the twins suggest that they wait until the morning to climb the mountain, but Ralph and Jack persist. The path is tougher now, rocky, with little outcroppings, and eventually they are confronted with an impossible barrier, a formidable cliff. Ralph says someone must go back to Piggy to let him know they will be gone until after dark. Jack makes fun of the chief for once again worrying about Piggy. Simon volunteers and heads off, while Ralph, furious at Jack, questions him about the island terrain so he can decide on a new path. Ralph, however, reconsiders, realizing it is getting dark, and wonders if they should continue, only to be taunted again by Jack. Exasperated and remembering Piggy's earlier comment, Ralph asks Jack directly, "Why do you hate me?" The only response is a stirring among the others.

Ralph leads the way, following a pig trail, until they see the stars in the sky. He suggests they go back to the others and climb the next day. The boys agree, except for Jack, who mocks Ralph for his cowardliness. Angered, Ralph decides he will climb, then says someone must accompany him, in case they find anything. Roger volunteers, and they set off. They are surrounded by darkness and choke when they get near the ashes from the fire. Ralph realizes how foolish they are, and when Jack says he will go on by himself Ralph finally decides to let him.

It does not take long for Jack to make it back. Shivering and with a voice that is hardly recognizable as his own, he tells the other two he has seen something bulging on the mountaintop, at which Ralph decides they will all go back up. Squeezed together, whispering, creeping on hands and knees, they come into view of the rocklike hump that suggests a large ape that lifts its head in the wind to show a ruined face. The three boys rush away in terror.

Chapter 8 opens at dawn the next day. Ralph, Jack, and Piggy are together. Ralph says they would never be able to fight the beast and ignores Jack when he offers his group of hunters to take up the challenge. Ralph adds a new twist: Since the creature is sitting right by the site of their fire, it must not want them to be rescued, and they cannot now build and maintain a fire. When Jack asks again whether his hunters can fight the beast, Ralph answers that they are only boys with sticks, angering Jack, who walks away.

The boys hear the conch, but this time Jack is the one blowing it. Rather than seeing this as a struggle for power, Ralph walks to the platform for the meeting and takes the shell from Jack. The two argue over which of them is running the meeting, until Ralph relents. Jack says that they all know that the three boys have seen the beast. With this, the gathered boys express their fears again about it coming from the ocean or even from the trees, stalking and hunting them. Jack agrees that the beast is a hunter and tells them that it cannot be killed.

Then Jack shifts the meeting in a new direction by turning on Ralph. He says that Ralph has called his hunters no good, that Ralph thinks they are cowards. He states that Ralph is the real coward, that he is not a hunter, that unlike Jack he is not a prefect (a student who has been given some disciplinary authority over others). With each point, Ralph interrupts to stand up for himself and set the record straight. Finally, Jack asks who in the group thinks Ralph should no longer be chief. The response is only silence. Jack, devastated, then puts down the shell, and as tears run down his face he says he is "not going to play any longer. Not with you." He announces he is going off by himself but that anyone who wants to hunt with him can do so. Ralph shouts at him as he leaves, but Jack yells back, enraged as the tears continue to flow. Ralph tells himself that Jack will come back, again not understanding the gravity of the situation.

Piggy starts to speak to the group, saying they do not need Jack Merridew and need to make their own plans. He, too, does not realize the damage caused by Jack's leaving. Simon interrupts, and despite jeers from the group, says they should go up the mountain. When Piggy questions why they would go back when the others had no success doing so, Simon whispers, "What else is there to do?" With another of his ideas dismissed, Simon then moves far away from the group.

Piggy, still supporting Ralph, says he knows Ralph is thinking that they must build a fire for a chance to be rescued. When Ralph disagrees, saying it is impossible to have a fire so close to the beast, Piggy says they will simply have to create a fire at the base of the island. The boys set to work, and Piggy starts the relocated signal fire with his one remaining lens. The "littluns" dance and sing as the flame grows, and a partylike atmosphere takes over. Ralph and Piggy talk about the type and size of the fire they should tend and discuss maintaining a schedule for taking care of it. As the "littluns" drift away, Ralph realizes how few older boys are left, while the more observant Piggy says he saw some of them go off in Jack's direction. To help rally their spirits, Piggy leaves with Sam and Eric, and they return to surprise Ralph with ripe fruit so they can have their own feast. Ralph, who has gradually become more aware of the others' activities, asks if Simon has left to climb the mountain, but Piggy only laughs, calling Simon cracked.

Simon has actually gone to his quiet spot hidden in the brush, where he kneels down and then sits, despite the heat. It is unclear if he has gone there to prepare himself to climb the mountain, to decide if he should attempt to, or to just be alone.

Farther down the beach, Jack now has his own small group of followers, the choirboys who have again donned their weathered black caps. He tells them he is the chief, that they will hunt and not concern themselves with the beast. Curiously, he adds, "We shan't dream so much down here. This is near the end of the island." He is possibly referring to the littluns, who have cried in their sleep, or to Ralph and Piggy who he may believe do too much thinking. The comment about their location indicates that they are far from the others and, at the same time, near the end, a more precarious spot and one also connoting that there is not much farther to go. In a more general way, Jack's statement could also indicate that their time on the island is limited, that the end of their time there will soon arrive.

Jack says he will get more of the older boys to join them, they will hunt a pig, have a feast, and leave some for the beast in the hopes that the offering will keep it from chasing them. They leave for the hunt immediately, and Jack quickly finds a group of unsuspecting pigs lounging in the shade. Displaying his blatant wickedness and lack of compassion, he intends to chase the sow that is resting with her piglets. Jack gives the order, and they aim and then throw their spears, which now have fire-hardened points. They race after the pig, which almost loses them at first, but because Jack is more experienced at hunting, he finds the animal's trail. They follow the boar as the afternoon goes on, "wedded to her in lust, excited by the long chase and the dropped blood." Finally they move in, and Jack and Roger deliver the fatal wounds, with Jack cutting her throat. Blood spouts, Jack laughs, and when he shows the boys his bloody palms, they laugh too.

Jack says he will invite the others to a feast, but Roger asks how he can do so since they do not have a fire. "We'll raid them," Jack says, not for a moment thinking there could be a more logical, peaceful solution. Before he can leave, though, they must make an offering to the beast, and Jack cuts off the pig's head and mounts it on a stick, near the pig's entrails, which have started to attract flies. He calls the head a gift, thus clarifying the meaning of the chapter's title, "Gift for the Darkness." All had stepped back when he mounted the head, and now all run away as fast as possible.

The narrative returns to Simon, who has remained hidden and is actually not far from the skewered sow's head. Her half-shut eyes are described as "dim with the infinite cynicism of adult life. They assured Simon that everything was a bad business." Simon agrees, apparently feeling as if the head is speaking to him. The head is repeatedly described as grinning and dripping. It sneers and seemingly cannot be ignored or pushed aside, since even as it drips, dismembered and dead, it still ominously communicates. The monstrosity is called the

Lord of the Flies, a translation of "Beelzebub," which is an alternate name for the devil, the ultimate evil.

The scene shifts to Ralph and Piggy lying in the sand by the fire, as dark clouds and thunder that sounds like a gun are portentously heard overhead. Ralph admits to Piggy that he is scared, that he does not understand why the others fail to recognize the importance of the fire, and that sometimes even he does not care about it. He wonders what would happen if he got to be like the others. Piggy says they would just have to go on, since that is what adults would do. Ralph suddenly realizes that he can slip like the others, lose his grip on his humanity. He is awakening to the idea that Piggy and Simon have already both grappled with, that the main beast to be scared of is the other boys on the island or even themselves. When Ralph asks what causes things to break apart, Piggy says he thinks it is Jack, and Ralph agrees; now they both recognize and identify a source of evil separate from themselves.

At this moment, boys with painted faces burst from the forest, and everyone but Ralph flees. Two of the painted boys take branches from the fire and leave, while three remain, one of them Jack, now completely naked except for a belt. Jack announces to all that his group is hunting, feasting, and having fun and that if the others want to join them they should let him know and he will decide if he will include them or not. He invites them to feast with his group that night and then before departing he shouts at the other two painted boys with him, who hesitate but then raise their spears and recite together, "The Chief has spoken." They leave.

Ralph and the others have a meeting. Ralph explains what happened but then forgets what else he wanted to say. With Piggy's help, he stumbles through his remaining few words, reminding the boys that the fire is the most important thing, since it can bring about their rescue. Even the youngest listeners realize the weakness in his words. Plus, missing from his address to the group is any clear plan or response to Jack being his own chief and looking for recruits.

Bill suggests that they go to the feast and tell the other group that keeping the fire going is too much for them. It is unclear if he thinks they should tell Jack's group that they need their help or if he thinks they should join Jack's group. He and the twins say it must be fun to hunt and be "savages." They are tempted by the meat. Ralph interrupts to ask why they cannot get their own meat, and the others reply that they do not want to go into the jungle. Even Piggy is enticed by the meat, as thunder sounds overhead once again, this time like a cannon.

The narrative then returns to Simon and the Lord of the Flies. The head tells the boy that it is the beast and that it is a part of him as well. Now it speaks in the voice of a schoolmaster. It warns Simon that he is not wanted, that they will have fun on the island, and warns him that if he tries anything, the others, including Ralph and Piggy, will destroy him. With this, Simon falls unconscious.

Chapter 9 is titled "A View to a Death" and opens with the clouds still building and "ready to explode." Simon, having experienced a bloody nose, soon fell asleep after being addressed by the dismembered head. Now he wakes up and says, "What else is there to do?" the same question he posed at the meeting after the three boys had reported seeing the beast on top of the mountain. Simon will climb the mountain by himself, despite being the one who is ridiculed for his physical weakness, who is too timid to talk at meetings, and who has just been threatened by the Lord of the Flies. As he climbs, he staggers at times from being so tired, but he continues until he gets near the humped figure and then close enough to determine what it actually is. He gets sick from seeing the parachutist's decomposed body but then untangles the parachute lines and sets them loose. The corpse sits beside him as Simon peers down at the boys, many if not all of whom appear to be far down the beach away from the platform. Then, Simon starts down the mountain, still staggering, to let the others know the true identity of the supposed beast.

Ralph and Piggy are still near their original camp, swimming. The first thing Ralph says is, "Bathing, that's the only thing to do." This line, similar to Simon's, points out a striking contrast. Simon is intent on doing something about the supposed beast at the top of the mountain, whereas Ralph is nearly at a loss over what they are to do and so utters his facetious line. Even though Ralph has come to recognize Piggy's value, he still teases him in the water, but, for once, Piggy adamantly fights back. Ralph backs off and asks where everyone is. Piggy, again revealed to be aware and observant of his surroundings, says the others have gone to Jack's party. Ralph has been outdone by both Piggy and Simon.

Ralph and Piggy head toward the party as well and approach the laughing, singing, relaxing boys, most of whom are nearly done eating. Jack is sitting in the center on a large log; he is still painted and now is also draped with garlands "like an idol." Ralph and Piggy are given meat and stand off to the side together, as Jack tells all to sit. He asks who wants to join his "tribe," but Ralph inserts that he is chief, and the two verbally spar. When some of the listening boys say they want to join Jack, Piggy leads Ralph away, warning that there is going to be trouble. Thunder sounds again, and great raindrops begin to fall. Ralph reminds them that he has shelters, but Jack does not. All are disturbed by the storm; some of the young boys run about screaming.

Jack yells for all to dance, and between bursts of lightning, Roger takes the part of the pig, charging at Jack, as the others grab spears, cooking spits, and firewood weapons. Piggy and Ralph join in, "eager to take a place in this demented but partly secure society. They were glad to touch the brown backs of the fence that hemmed in the terror and made it governable." The group takes up the killing chant, and Roger moves out of the circle to become a hunter rather than the hunted.

Simon crawls out of the forest into the group of yelling boys and tries to scream over them about the dead parachutist. He breaks out of the circle, but the hunters chase after him and are out of control, forcing Simon into the role of beast. They "leapt on to the beast, screamed, struck, bit, tore. There were no words, and no movements but the tearing of teeth and claws." Torrents of rain surge down. The struggling group on the sand breaks up, and the boys stagger away, leaving "the beast" there, unmoving, near the sea edge, where "already its blood was staining the sand."

Swept away by the storm, the parachutist falls from the mountain, landing near the boys, who scream and run off. The great parachute canvas and its dead passenger finally are blown out to sea.

Near midnight, the storm has ended, the sky and water are clear, and "strange, moonbeam-bodied creatures with fiery eyes" are near Simon's broken body. His head lit with brightness, his "cheek silvered" and the line of his shoulder "became sculptured marble." His body advances into the sea.

Golding has stated that Simon is the novel's Christ figure, misunderstood, laughed at, contemplative, solitary, who has a message but is killed. In Golding's book, though, the great message makes it to no one, and a new faith or system of beliefs is not created as a result of this boy's life and death.

Chapter 10 again opens with Piggy and Ralph. Ralph, with a swollen cheek that has reduced his eye to a slit and a scarred knee, limps toward Piggy, who is sitting on the platform, a place of democracy, order, and problem solving that now seems emptied of the ceremonial power it once possessed. Piggy tells Ralph that the only ones left are some of the "littluns" and the twins, who are collecting wood. Ralph sits on the platform as well but faces the conch and the chief's seat rather than sitting in that designated spot. Ralph whispers something that Piggy cannot hear and then repeats, "Simon." Piggy just nods, and they fall silent again.

Ralph caresses the light gleaming conch and asks yet again what they are going to do. He laughs sharply at the thought of calling a meeting. When he stops, he speaks again of Simon, saying bluntly that they murdered him. However, no matter what Ralph says, Piggy tries to rationalize. He warns Ralph not to admit to the twins that he and Ralph were took part in the dance. When the twins appear with wood for the fire, they say they got lost in the forest after the feast. Piggy says he and Ralph left early, and the twins say they did the same. Ralph is silent and lets the others weave their own stories; all have been shaken by the experience, but apparently no one is able to speak of the incident directly.

Meanwhile, Jack's group has its own reaction to the horrible events. Jack has started to get the boys to set up a protective cave at the place where the main island meets the jutting Castle Rock. He reminds the boys that the beast may try to break in, like it crawled in on them the other night in its disguise. A boy tries to clarify what happened, but Jack insists that they did not kill the beast: "No! How could we—kill—it?" While it was disturbing to hear Piggy, the twins, and Ralph deny Simon's homicide, much less participating in it, in Jack's group the situation is much worse, for no one mentions Simon's name. Jack also continues to encourage ancient pagan ritual, reminding them that they must leave a present for the beast after a hunt. Again, one of the boys questions how they will make a fire, revealing Jack to be remiss once again in fulfilling his tribe's basic needs.

At that moment, Ralph and the others are trying to make a fire, although it proves difficult, because everything is still wet from the storm. They think about getting rescued, and Ralph considers the figure in the parachute; this is the first time it is revealed that anyone had seen much of the figure that had floated down by them. He says that Simon had been trying to tell them something about a dead man, but none of the others around Ralph seem to hear. Even he does not seem to have pieced together the entire mystery.

Since the two are disheartened about tending the fire with so few boys left in their group and since the logs and other fuel are so wet, they decide to forget about the fire for the night and to start it again in the morning. They go to sleep, and Ralph dreams of being home but must alter the dream when he realizes that some of the places he had once considered idyllic because they are naturally wild no longer have any appeal for him. He is awakened by Piggy, who says he has been making a disturbing noise, and the two see that the twins are fighting with each other in their sleep. It used to be that only the youngest boys suffered such disturbances.

Ralph is again awakened by Piggy, who says he hears something. Ralph hears nothing at first but then does, and the two boys become frightened. A horrid voice just outside the shelter whispers for Piggy to come out. Ralph tells him not to answer, and as the voice calls again, Piggy has an asthma attack.

Shortly the creatures outside invade the shelter, and a brawl ensues in the darkness. The shelter collapsing only increases the chaos, and the dark figures escape.

When the remaining boys pull themselves out and check on Piggy, they realize his breathing is less labored. All have been battered, and when they tell their own tales about what they did to the enemy, Ralph realizes they have, in fact, also fought one another in the confusion. Piggy says he thought they came for the conch shell, but when Ralph checks, it is still sitting by the platform, ready for another meeting to help bring about some structure and order. Piggy knows what they really wanted though, since his glasses are missing. Without them he cannot see, and now he turns to Ralph and asks a question similar to the one that Ralph had recently asked Piggy: "[W]hat am I going to do?" The chapter's title, "The Shell and the Glasses," indicates the most important tools on the island, but while losing the shell would be a disturbing event for Ralph's group, the loss of the glasses means they can no longer start a fire—their only hope for rescue. Piggy has also become notably weakened.

The boys who have taken the glasses return to their camp, turning cartwheels as they go. This immediately draws to mind the image of Ralph who early in the book took such delight in the island's riches and its lack of adults that he would stand on his head. These cartwheeling boys, however, are delighting in having power over the others. Nonetheless, since Jack never felt that keeping a fire was a priority, with him now in possession of the valuable glasses, the boys' chance of getting rescued potentially drops significantly.

In **chapter 11**, Ralph blows on ashes to see if there might still be enough spark to start a new fire, but there is none. At Piggy's prompting, Ralph calls an assembly and then prompts Piggy to speak first. He suggests that they must figure out a way to get his glasses back, that Ralph is the only one on the island who has accomplished anything and that he must tell them what to do. Ralph reminds the group of how Jack had let the fire go out before, just when a ship had been passing. He alludes to Simon's death being Jack's fault as well. When pressed for a plan, Ralph says they should clean themselves up like they used to be to show they are not savages and then approach the other group. The twins agree but not totally, saying they will bring swords with them as well.

Piggy asks what adults will think of the events on the island. This demonstrates he believes they will be rescued some day and also shows his lack of understanding that they are trapped on the island because of the violence of adults. He is bolder than Ralph here, since he calls Simon's death murder, and he mentions the young boy who died in the fire when they first arrived on the island. He says he will go to Jack Merridew with the conch in his hand. He recites what he will say, explaining that he will tell Jack he must give his glasses back because it is the right thing to do. He is trembling, and tears fall from his eyes. We realize that his logic will not work on Jack and that his own fear will make the confrontation impossible. Ralph, nonetheless, says Piggy can try his plan and that he and the twins will go with him.

The meeting is concluded, so the four boys can eat and prepare to leave. Again Ralph says the boys should "be like we were" and that they should wash and possibly comb their hair. But the boys have other ideas, and Ralph gives in, realizing that it is impossible to look the way he would like them to. He possibly realizes as well that no matter how they look, they cannot go back to the way they were. The twins, once again off track in the discussion, suggest that they should paint their faces, but Ralph is adamantly against this and sharply tells that they will not do it. He struggles to remember what is important—the fire's smoke that can get them rescued. This lack of memory shows that he is weakened mentally as well as physically. Piggy chimes in, and Ralph berates him, angry that Piggy is finishing his thoughts as if he cannot remember them himself, which actually seems to be the case. The twins look more closely at Ralph.

The four set off, with Ralph limping along first, visually impaired because of the hot haze, his long hair, and his swollen face that presses his eye partially closed. He seems unaware that this latest plan contains the potential for tragedy. The boys seem to instinctively know that the others will be at

Castle Rock (the title of the chapter), a spit of land with a ledge surrounding its rock and red rock pinnacles far above. As they pursue the precarious route, they are forty feet above the water, and Piggy questions the safety of the situation.

From the pinnacle comes a fake war cry and someone shouts down to ask who they are. Ralph sees Roger way above him and shouts back that he can see who they are and therefore is "silly" for asking. Ralph blows the conch shell and says he is calling an assembly. The "savages" guarding the area do not move. They snicker slightly, and Ralph repeats that he is calling an assembly. Finally, Ralph asks where Jack is. They tell him he is hunting and has ordered that no one be allowed in. Ralph explains why he and the others have come, and his words are met with laughter.

Jack, back from his hunt, comes up behind Ralph and asks what he wants. Piggy cries out in fear, and the boys on the rock jeer loudly. Ralph says Jack must return Piggy's glasses, that it was a "dirty trick" to have stolen them like a thief, and that they would have given Jack fire if he had only asked for it.

Jack rushes at Ralph to stab his chest, but Ralph deflects it. After additional strikes, there is an unstated mutual agreement to not use the spears for stabbing. Breathing heavily, the boys now part and taunt one another. Even in his vulnerable state, Piggy reminds Ralph that their goal is to get the glasses and be able to restart their fire. Ralph realizes that he is right, relaxes his tight muscles, and rests his spear butt on the ground. He restates that they have come for the glasses, and again Piggy whispers that they are important because of the fire. Reminded, Ralph tells the others of the fire's importance, but they laugh, which only increases his anger. Calling them "painted fools," Ralph notes that he, Piggy, and the twins are not enough to keep the fire going, and his announcement is followed by silence.

The direct, logical approach and the attempt at negotiation expectedly fails. Jack orders his men to grab the twins and tie them up. While at first they hesitate, they then do as commanded, surging with newfound power. Jack, as would be expected of a devil, attempts to strike Ralph from behind, but Ralph fends off the attack. Ralph then loses his temper and screams that Jack is "a beast and a swine and a bloody, bloody thief!" Calling Jack a beast is fitting, since the beast has come to symbolize evil and has provoked great fear among the children. Calling Jack a swine serves to demean him and reduce him to a helpless, hunted animal, forcing him out of his previously established role as powerful hunter. Identifying him as a "bloody, bloody thief" is appropriate because of his burglary not only of the glasses but of the boys' goodness and innocence. While "bloody" is used in England as a curse or for emphasis, it also is significant here because Jack is happy to kill pigs and was also partly responsible for Simon's death. He has blood on his hands from more than one source.

Ralph and Jack rush at each other, using their fists to the sounds of the "shrill cheering of the tribe." Again, Piggy interrupts. He shouts that he has the conch, and the boys fall silent, showing the power of the symbol even in the worst of circumstances. In the silence, Ralph hears a stone fall past his head; Roger has thrown it, while his other hand is on the stick serving as a lever under a huge rock. Piggy yells at them for "acting like a crowd of kids," which, of course, is ironic, since this is what they are. When they boo, he is still able to silence them by holding up the shell. He offers them alternatives—between being a "pack of Indians" or being sensible like Ralph, and then between having rules and agreeing or hunting and killing. Ralph adds to the choices as well, but Jack's yells interrupt him. Jack has now backed into the spear-yielding tribe, and they appear ready to charge.

Ralph and Piggy seem minute against the throng. "The storm of sound beat at them," Golding writes, "an incantation of hatred. High overhead, Roger, with a sense of delirious abandonment, leaned all his weight on the lever." Ralph hears the boulder coming and flings himself down. Piggy is hit. The conch shell shatters into pieces, and Piggy is hurled down the 40-foot drop. When he lands, his skull opens and releases "something," signifying the loss of his intelligence and guidance that had served the castaways well. His body is immediately sucked into the sea.

All are silent, except Jack. He screams wildly and takes credit for the horrific death, warning Ralph that he will get the same treatment. He hollers that Ralph no longer has a tribe or a conch and that he, Jack, is the chief. Still, it is not enough that Ralph has seemingly lost everything. Jack wants him dead. He launches his spear at Ralph, and it slashes past his ribs. The screaming tribe moves forward; two more spears fly by Ralph, and he runs, making it into the dense forest. Jack, the new chief, orders his charges back to the fort. Then, he turns to the twins and tells them they must join the tribe. He pokes Sam with a spear repeatedly, and then Roger relieves him of the task.

Chapter 12, the last in the book, is titled "Cry of the Hunters" and, unlike many of the other chapter titles, it is not long before its significance is made clear, although the chapter title gains additional resonance at the end of the book. When the chapter opens, Ralph is hiding but is still relatively close to Castle Rock, and as it gets darker he sneaks out of the ferns. He smells the roasting pig and realizes that, while the others are feasting, he will be safe. He toys with the notion that perhaps the tribe will actually leave him alone for the rest of their time on the island, but when he thinks about Simon and Piggy and Jack's hatred of him, he realizes the "savages" will eventually come after him. He goes to find fruit and then works his way back toward the rock at the end of the island.

Along the way, he encounters the pig's skull that "grinned" on the stick and "seemed to jeer at him cynically." Filled with anger and fear, Ralph strikes at it until it finally breaks into two pieces, with its grin notably wider as a result. He takes the spear that had been holding up the head and backs away as he keeps his eyes on it. He appears more naïve than Simon, who while fearful of the head recognized its message of evil and that it could not be destroyed.

As Ralph gets closer to Castle Rock, he hears the boys' hunting chant. He discerns the figures of the twins in the sentry post and is greatly disappointed to see them as part of this ghastly tribe. Not to be defeated, however, Ralph moves closer and calls to them. When they realize it is Ralph, they tell him he must leave and even fiercely wave a spear.

Finally, the twins tell Ralph that they were wounded and forced to be part of the tribe, that Roger and "the chief" hate Ralph and are going "to do" him. They will all hunt him the following day, and they explain that they will use signals as they search the island, spreading out in a great line across it. Ralph asks what will happen if he is found, and he gets no direct answer, as he hangs over the rock where Piggy fell and died far below. The twins warn him about Jack and Roger, and when they hear someone coming they fear that it is Roger checking to be sure they are doing their assigned job. Quickly, they throw Ralph a piece of meat. As he finds a place to hide in the ferns and grass, he hears Sam and Eric yelling on the top of the rock, panicked and in pain.

In the morning, a hunter's cry wakes Ralph, who crawls deep into the ferns and thicket, on the way glimpsing the legs of a "savage" coming toward him. The boy beats at the ferns around Ralph but continues on, signaling the others near him. For some time, Ralph hears no more cries. He realizes as he looks around that the great rock that had sent Piggy to his death is actually now helping him, since it has created a secure hiding space.

From his secluded spot, Ralph hears Roger and Jack ask one of the boys, "Are you certain?" Roger threatens the boy and hits him, and Ralph assumes the victim is one of the twins. Roger and Jack ask if this is where Ralph said he would hide, and this time a voice answers with a definite yes. Ralph tenses but then realizes he is still safe in the thick growth, that even if someone wormed his way in Ralph would have the advantage.

From the top of the rock, Ralph hears Jack's voice and then soon after hears the sound of a rock thundering down the cliff face. The thicket area is hit, but only broken twigs and leaves fall on Ralph. The boys cheer. Now Ralph fears the consequences as he hears the boys straining to push another enormous rock. Once released, its great force shoots Ralph into the air, and the soil only a few feet from him is wrenched up along with roots, stumps, and sticks.

Ralph then hears whispering close by. There is snickering, an objection, more snickering, and then smoke appears. Ralph runs. He tries to decide the best course of action and repeatedly wishes he had time to think. He concludes he can either climb a tree or run through the line of boys and then run back, losing them. He has seen pigs escape that way, he thinks. The observation only emphasizes his persistent optimism as well as his near helplessness, for while the plan can work, there also have been pigs that have been killed, and Jack has evolved into more of an expert hunter.

Ralph sees his third option as hiding. He hears a hunter's cry close by, gets up from his temporary resting spot, and takes off again. By mistake, he runs into the open and is directly in front of the broken pig skull that he had knocked off its skewer and broken. It still lies in the sand "jeering," and its enormous grin is a dreadful reminder that evil persists and may ultimately triumph.

Now out of the brambles and trees, Ralph sees more smoke and realizes the fire the boys have created is huge. He decides his best strategy is to hide, and after some searching he finds the hidden spot where Simon had so often retreated and was never found. For the reader, this brings to mind the fact that Simon told Ralph he thought Ralph would be saved. Ralph can hear the fire getting closer; the fruit trees, their primary food source, will soon be destroyed, and as animals run from the heat and smoke, the boys' other main source of food, the wild boars, may perish as well. With a hunter suddenly closing in on Ralph's location, he readies himself with his spear, which he realizes is sharpened at both ends just like Roger's, showing there is no escaping the island savagery. The hunter comes closer, finds Ralph's hidden spot, but at first is unable to see clearly inside. Ralph sees that the boy is ready to poke in his spear, and Ralph emerges from his hiding spot in a burst of fear, strength, and anger. He pushes the boy over, but others are already moving in. He races from them and the rushing fire, stumbles, and right before he falls, sees a shelter erupt in flames; the shelters were one of the few symbols of civilization they had on the island and which he was largely responsible for building. Thrown to the ground, Ralph rolls over and over in the sand at the water's edge.

As he forces himself to his feet, he looks up into a huge peaked cap, presumably of one of the choirboys. In the next sentence, however, Golding reveals the cap's peak to be white, while the choirboys' hats are black. He then offers a description of the rest of the cap as well as of a uniform and gun. Again, like the shelter, these are symbols of civilization, although the presence of the gun indicates that, even in a civilized sphere, a weapon is needed. Finally, after the description of these items, it is revealed that the person wearing them is a naval officer, who is accompanied by others in boats behind him. Ralph responds to him shyly, and the officer "inspected the little scarecrow. . . . The kid," he thinks, "needed a bath, a haircut, a nose-wipe and a good deal of ointment." Immediately, Ralph is transformed from the chief back into a little boy.

The officer "grinned cheerfully" and says they saw the smoke coming from the island. Smoke, what Ralph has been continually telling the others was imperative for their rescue, does in fact bring it about, yet, ironically, this smoke has been created by Jack in an act of reckless aggression. The officer jokingly asks Ralph if they were having a war, and when Ralph nods affirmatively the officer, still believing the boys were playing, asks, "Nobody killed, I hope? Any dead bodies?" When Ralph tells him two are dead, the officer looks at him carefully, asks him the question again, and then realizes this is the truth.

"[T]he whole island was shuddering with flame," Golding writes, the palms at the platform, yet another symbol of order, quickly engulfed. More boys appear on the shore, and, when the officer asks who the boss is, Ralph loudly says that he is, while behind him, Golding writes, another "little boy" with red hair almost announces that he is. The officer says that since the boys are all British, he would have expected that they "would have been able to put up a better show." Again, the language of make-believe is being invoked, as if the boys had not been trying to survive but had been playing or acting out a scene; this seems somewhat appropriate, though, since in some way their experience on the island has seemed unreal, a daydream or invented scenario.

The officer is ready to take the boys from the island, but his comment about how they behaved brings Ralph to tears. He shakes with sobs, and others join in. "Ralph wept for the end of innocence, the darkness of man's heart, and the fall through the air of the true, wise friend called Piggy," Golding writes.

The book ends, some have criticized, with a gimmick that saves Ralph just in time. Yet the ending, however forced it may seem, reminds the reader that the evil that has taken place here has all been at the hands of little boys. Also, ironically, the boys are being rescued from this evil realm by an armed ship that will bring them back to civilization, which has been in the throes of its own horrid war.

Critical Views

DAVID ANDERSON ON GOLDING'S DIFFICULT CHRISTIANITY

Golding is a maker of myths, not a debater of doctrines: his concern is the creation of theologically significant experience rather than theological statement. He descries realities of human behavior and consciousness which theological statements indicate but do not enact. What is it like to experience the fall from innocence into sin? What is it like to experience damnation? To create an idolatrous god in the image of man or beast? To be stretched on the rack of such contraries as life and death, sacred and profane love, the self and the other? And, more tentatively, what would it be like to experience atonement and resurrection? These are some of the themes of Golding's novels, the stuff of existence upon which theological reflection operates. Doing theology does not mean spinning abstract formulations of nonempirical reality out of one's head. However remote and academic the theologian may seem, he asserts that his discourse has been prompted by events and experience judged to be of cosmic significance and giving access to the way things ultimately are. This process can also operate in reverse, when the creative imagination reenacts, in the form of myth, the immediate experience presupposed by doctrinal formulation. Such reversal can go further: it can enact experience which brings theological statement under reappraisal and challenges its assumptions (the early stories in Genesis and the Book of Job are biblical examples). Events and new knowledge can cause a disorientation calling for new theological solutions. How far a basic doctrine can be qualified and reinterpreted while remaining the same doctrine is a particularly perplexing question today. To give a specific example, which brings us near the center of Golding's concern, we may ask whether the traditional Christian doctrine of Original Sin is still the same doctrine when its basis in the story of the Fall is recognized as myth, not history, and when Original Sin is interpreted not as the result of a primal rebellious act, but as an inevitable concomitant of man's existential condition. It can be said that the doctrine is no longer the same if it leaves God out—if, for instance, human wickedness and misery are attributed to prerational drives deriving from man's animal ancestry which in time he will outgrow. The Christian doctrine of Original Sin is about the rupture of man's relationship with God; it is not about the incompleteness of evolutionary development. One factor that makes Golding a Christian writer is his recognition of the difference between these two anthropologies and his siding with the theological rather than the biological version, though he also recognizes that the terms in which the Christian doctrine becomes existentially significant today will require a reformulation of orthodoxy. . . .

In Golding's novels the absence of God from the center of human consciousness is explored. Such absence can take two forms. In one, God is absent simply because he is unnecessary. The only meanings are those which man himself creates, and the puzzles and predicaments of existence are solved by human rationality scientifically applied. . . .

One reason Golding is a novelist rather than a polemicist is that he feels the attractiveness of [the] humanist claim. Ralph mourns the death of his "true, wise friend called Piggy" (Golding has denied that this is his own judgment, but it has its own level of authenticity in the novel). . . . If only he *could* drive back the mystery until it disappeared and order his life by rational principles and techniques!

But with another form of the absence of God the rationalism of Piggy and [Nick] Shales [a character from *Free Fall*] is powerless to deal. The true God is absent, but his place has been taken by a distorted, demonic image. Golding enacts experience which reveals that the rationalist hope is based upon a reductionist account of human awareness. Man is haunted by the supernatural, by a reality that transcends his own power of mastery and order and presents itself as a rival contender in the power game, requiring some kind of propitiation. The boys on the island . . . are afraid of devils; . . . The demons are the reason the attempt to live by law and reason is "no go," why things are what they are. The consequences are murder, cannibalism, madness, despair.

It is possible to argue, as Piggy does, that demons do not exist and that a cool rationalism will expose the deception. The impotence of this program is, Golding shows, due to the fact that man comes to cherish the demons because they endorse his own will to power. The demons are objectifications of lust masquerading as ultimate reality, and man needs the demons because they are the means by which he writes himself large upon the universe. . . .

Golding is not one of those simple-minded evangelists who see religion as an easy solution to the puzzles of existence. Indeed, the official representatives of religion come off badly in the novels. The choir-boys in *Lord of the Flies* become horrifying hunters. . . .

Men do terrible things when they act in the name of religion and claim divine authority for their programs. Precisely because it points to a transcendent reality, religion can tempt a man into the belief that he can himself attain transcendence, that he can climb out of the relativism and finitude of his condition and attain absolute truth. Here, indeed, we find the deepest paradox of human consciousness: that man touches the fringe of the eternal, that he glimpses the infinite, and yet knows himself to be subject to temporality. So it is that he builds towers of Babel from which to survey his condition *sub specie aeternitatis* and claim equality with God. But the towers are never high enough. Like the original tower, they are unfinished, witnessing to the inevitable limitations of human endeavor and to the hubris which has attempted to go beyond them. . . .

Human pride is one aspect of what Christian orthodoxy means by Original Sin. The importance of this doctrine lies in its recognition of evil in the best of human actions. We do not require a doctrine to remind us of man's violence and barbarism; what we do need is a doctrine that questions his noblest dreams and his most sublime inventions. Only man's recognition of his fallenness, of the distance that separates him from God, can safeguard him from the attribution of absolute authority to his programs. Golding has shown what happens when a man forgets his fallenness. . . .

Golding's novels are a great deal more than anything one can say about them. An essay that attempts to draw out meanings is bound to simplify, to ignore richness and density, to fasten on this part of the content rather than that, to treat the novels as problems to be solved rather than experiences to be entered. Inevitably, too, one's response is affected by one's own interpretation of life, and one tends to find what one expects. . . . I have tried to show that the Christian frame is more inclusive than its rivals, though this is not to say that every image and event has a counterpart in Christian doctrine. I have also suggested that Golding's work operates in some respects as a critique of Christian understanding, especially of those contemporary forms of it which discard the supernatural dimension of traditional belief and offer only a phenomenological version of reality. Golding gives us new ways of imaging Christian doctrine, mythological enactments which are also in an important sense the modern equivalents of the archetypal stories in Genesis. And what he reformulates is recognizably the mainstream of Christian tradition, not some reduction of it which is hardly distinguishable from its atheistic alternatives. At least Golding's doctrine of man is worth disagreeing with. What cannot be denied is the depth and seriousness of his presentation and the sharp reality of our response to it.

KATHLEEN WOODWARD DISCUSSES THE CAPACITY FOR EVIL IN CHILDREN

As a fable *Lord of the Flies* may be about the evil in the human heart, but as a novel it is about the frightening potential of children for violence. This is one of the complicated and fascinating effects of the book. The adult world may indeed be marked by extreme brutality—we remember intermittently that an atomic war is in process—but it seems for the moment infinitely preferable to the violent anarchy of children. For in the course of the narrative our suspension of disbelief is so perfectly manipulated by Golding that we temporarily forget that these characters are in fact children and respond to them as if they were adults. Thus, when they are rescued by a naval officer at the end of the story, and we recognize with a shock that they are children after all, we are willing to accept anything but this, even an atomic war, which now seems less savage than the violent obsessions of young Jack and his followers.

True, the conclusion of *Lord of the Flies* is ironic, a kind of frame which sets the fable in place. As Golding asks elsewhere, commenting on the ending of the story, "The officer, having interrupted a manhunt, prepares to take the children off the island in a cruiser which will presently be hunting its enemy in the same implacable way. And who will rescue the adult and his cruiser?" But this is not the only effect of the ending. We welcome with uncomplicated relief the figure of authority. We conclude that children require strict supervision and constant discipline, for without these, they pose a serious threat to the adult world.

Doris Lessing has written about this in her fine novel *Memoirs of a Survivor* (1975), which is also set in a future postwar period. As the narrator, who is an adult, admits, "At the sight of children, I was afraid. And I realized 'in a flash'—another one!—that I, that everybody had come to see all children as, simply, terrifying." The children form angry survival bands. How can they be dealt with? One character concludes that "the only way to cope with the 'kids' was to separate them and put them into households in ones and twos." This is how to deal with the enemy—divide and conquer. In Golding's most recent novel, *Darkness Visible*, which is as sophisticated and phantasmagorical as *Lord of the Flies* is not, children also manifest this capacity for perverse behavior. The young Sophy, a beautiful child much admired for her angelic charm, reflects malevolently about killing her twin sister, whom she thinks receives more attention than she does. Both sisters grow up to be terrorists who not only fantasize about the politics of violence, but practice it. All of this resonates with our contemporary experience. In the newspapers we read of children not yet ten who beat up the elderly, of young babysitters who torture their charges in microwave ovens, of children who try to kill their parents, as the following newspaper clipping about an incident in Slidell, Louisiana, shows:

> Two girls discussed ways of killing their sleeping parents after a family argument, then set fire to their trailer home, police say.
>
> The parents were in a suburban New Orleans hospital Sunday with severe burns over 45% of their bodies.
>
> "They discussed shooting, stabbing, cutting their heads off and finally decided on fire," a sheriff's spokesman said.
>
> Deputies said the murder was planned after the girls, aged 9 and 13, got into an argument with their parents Friday.
>
> The girls were booked with aggravated arson and the attempted murders of Truett Simpson, 51, and his wife, Glenda, 42, who were rescued from their burning mobile home about 3 A.M. Saturday. It was first thought that the daughters died in the fire, but they were found later in New Orleans.

This is evil, an action, like Jack's, so reprehensible that we cannot imagine a punishment for it. As our society grows more severely age-segregated, the generations come to regard each other as alien—the elderly are strangers to the middle-aged, children perceive their parents as belonging to another species, parents are threatened by their children. Much of the power of reading Golding's novel today rests here: the fear of the child as a violent other, virulent in itself, not a mere analogy for adult brutality (which we know better and accept more easily), but a potential enemy who turns, perversely, the screw.

Arnold Kruger Takes a New Look at the Character of Simon

It is an accepted critical truism that the character of Simon in William Golding's *Lord of the Flies* is an analogue of Christ; that

Simon's holy, saintly, self-sacrificial behavior is an exemplar of all that is most high and good in human life; that he is an epiphanic figure. And his death, a communal execution, so echoes the Crucifixion that the correspondence seems complete. An alert reading of the text, though, together with an examination of the biblical references to both Christ and his apostle Simon Peter, gives a somewhat different view of Simon. On the preponderance of this evidence, I suggest that Golding's character is actually an analogue of Christ's apostle Simon Peter.

The distinction between the roles of Christ and his apostle may seem a fine one, but the essential elements of the difference are important both to the story and its underlying allegory. I say this on the basis of Golding's overt Christian faith. He says in his book of essays *A Moving Target*: "Of man and God. We have come to it, have we not? I believe in God" (192).

The figure of Christ is commonly conflated with that of any especially spiritual character—anyone who evidences saintliness, selflessness, and undiscriminating love for his fellow creatures. This, of course, is what Simon does, as in the scene in which he feeds the "littluns": "Simon found for them the fruit they could not reach, pulled off the choicest from up in the foliage, passed them back down to the endless, outstretched hands" (61). A nice image of selfless caring, but also an observance of Christ's injunction to his apostle Simon Peter: "Jesus said to Simon Peter, 'Simon, son of John, do you love me more than these?' He said to him, 'Yes, Lord; you know that I love you.' He said to him, 'Feed my lambs'" (KJV, John 21.15). This picture of Simon/Simon Peter placing ripe fruit into the hands of children, is clearly an allusion to the nurturing and proselytizing roles of Christ's apostles within the Church; as Simon Peter himself says: "Feed the flock of God which is among you . . ." (1 Pet. 5.2).

Another example of the essential difference between Simon and Christ occurs at the beginning of the novel, when Simon is introduced as "the choirboy who had fainted . . . smil[ing] pallidly . . ." (23). His personality and behavior bear a strong resemblance to that of the biblical Simon Peter, who is scolded by Christ when he says: "Simon, are you asleep? . . . the spirit indeed is willing, but the flesh is weak" (Mark 14.37). Simon's "choirboy" position further reinforces his secondary status and might be compared with that of Simon Peter, an apostle in attendance on Christ.

But the central cause of the confusion of the Simon character with Christ is Simon's murder at the hands of a mob while trying to deliver them from fear of "the beast." The murder does evoke Christ's Crucifixion, but only superficially—as the murder of any spiritual figure would. In fact, most of the apostles and many ordinary Christians of that period died on crosses and gibbets, and in arenas—all of them murdered by mobs. The giveaway in Simon's case is that he died "crying out something about a dead man on a hill" (168), much as the biblical Simon Peter must have. That is, the likely cause of his death was his proselytizing, which he would have continued even on his cross, "crying out" the Christian message of sacrifice and redemption. The "dead man on a hill" is, of course, Christ on Golgotha, dying for our sins; the phrase itself, with its evocation of ignorant confusion and mockery, dramatizes the incredulity with which the Christian experience is often received.

Simon's death and its consequences are much different from those of Christ's. And the scene of Simon's apotheosis, after his death when "his cheek silvered and the turn of his shoulder became sculptured marble . . . and his coarse hair was dressed with brightness" (170), is a lovely, lyric metaphor of the promise of death for all men in Christ:

> Lo! I tell you a mystery. We shall not all sleep, but we shall all be changed, in a moment, in the twinkling of an eye, at the last trumpet. For the trumpet will sound, and the dead will be raised imperishable, and we shall be changed . . . (1 Cor. 15.51–52)

Although Simon falls short of Christ's perfection, he remains a witness to the higher reaches of the human spirit.

James R. Baker Considers Golding, Huxley, and Modernity

Surely we have heard enough about William Golding's *Lord of the Flies*. Published in 1954, it rapidly gained popularity in England, then in America, then in translation throughout Europe, Russia, and Asia, until it became one of the most familiar and studied tales of the century. In the 1960s it was rated an instant classic in the literature of disillusionment that grew out of the latest great war, and we felt certain it was the perfect fable (more fable than fiction) that spelled out what had gone wrong in that dark and stormy time and what might devastate our future.

But in the postwar generation a new spirit was rising, a new wind blowing on campus, a new politics forming to oppose the old establishment and its failures. Golding, proclaimed "Lord of the Campus" by *Time* magazine (64) in 1962, was soon found wanting—an antique tragedian, a pessimist, a Christian moralist who would not let us transcend original sin and the disastrous history of the last 50 years. . . .

The identity assigned to Golding during these years was not substantially altered by his later work. . . . He remained the man who wrote *Lord of the Flies*, the man who felt he had to protest his designation as pessimist even in his Nobel speech of 1983 (Nobel Lecture 149–50). Have we been entirely fair? Golding's reputation, like that of any artist, was created not simply by what he wrote or intended but also by the prevailing mentality of his readership, and often a single work will be selected by that readership as characteristic or definitive. Writer and reader conspire to sketch a portrait of the artist that may or may not endure. . . .

In 1962 I began correspondence with Golding in preparation for a book on his work (*William Golding: A Critical Study*). My thesis . . . was that the structure and spirit of *Lord of the Flies* were modeled on Euripidean tragedy, specifically *The Bacchae*, and that the later novels also borrowed character and structure from the ancient tragedians. Golding's response:

With regard to Greek, you are quite right that I go to that literature for its profound engagement with first and last things. But though a few years ago it was true I'd read little but Greek for twenty years, it's true no longer. The Greek is still there and I go back to it when I feel like that; now I must get in touch with the contemporary scene, and not necessarily the literary one; the scientific one perhaps. (Baker and Golding, letter 12 August 1965)

Science? What could he mean? . . .

I interviewed Golding in 1982. . . . Had there been a "classic revolt," I asked, against his father's scientific point of view? After some defense of the father's complexity of mind, the conclusion was clear: "But I do think that during the formative years I did feel myself to be in a sort of rationalist atmosphere against which I kicked" (130). I also asked whether he felt he belonged to the long line of English writers who, especially since Darwin, had taken scientist and the scientific account of things into their own work—a line running from Tennyson and including among others Hardy, Wells, Huxley, Snow, Durrell, and Fowles. . . .

Since Golding's death in 1993 his work has gone into partial eclipse, as he himself predicted. While we wait for recovery, if it ever comes, we should adjust our accounts. We shall find that much of the fiction was oriented and directly influenced by his knowledge of science and that there is an evolution from the extreme negativism of *Lord of the Flies* toward greater respect for the scientist and scientific inquiry. The much discussed sources for the dark fable lie in Golding's experience of the war, in his connection with Lord Cherwell's research into explosives, in the use of the atomic bombs on Japan, in the postwar revelations of the Holocaust and the horrors of Stalinist Russia—quite enough to bring on the sense of tragic denouement and, as he said in "A Moving Target" (163), "grief, sheer grief" as inspiration, if that is the proper word.

Was there a contemporary literary source or precedent on which he could build his own account of the failure of humanity and the likelihood of atomic apocalypse? . . . In an address titled "Utopias and Antiutopias" he comes, inevitably, to Aldous Huxley:

> As the war clouds darkened over Europe he and some of our most notable poets removed themselves to the new world. . . . There Huxley continued to create what we may call antiutopias and utopias with the same gusto, apparently, for both kinds. One antiutopia is certainly a disgusting job and best forgotten. . . . Yet I owe his writings much myself, I've had much enjoyment from them—in particular release from a certain starry-eyed optimism which stemmed from the optimistic rationalism of the nineteenth century. The last utopia he attempted which was technically and strictly a utopia and ideal state, *Island* (1962), is one for which I have a considerable liking and respect. (181) . . .

Huxley was the near-contemporary (17 years separated them) so much admired in the early stage of Golding's efforts, and he was quite like Golding—knowledgeable about science and scientists, yet dedicated to literature, intent upon spiritual experience and a search for an acceptable religious faith. Huxley's skeptical views were an update on H. G. Wells and his rather quaint "scientific humanism," a faith fading in Huxley's mind and lost to Golding and many of his generation. . . .

In Golding's island society the man of reason, the scientist, is represented in the sickly, myopic child Piggy, the butt of schoolboy gibes, but unfortunately many readers and most critics have failed to understand his limitations and thus his function in the allegory. This may be explained, in part, by the uncritical adoration of the scientist in our society, but another factor is the misunderstanding found in the prestige introduction by E. M. Forster in the first American edition of *Lord of the Flies* and subsequently held before our eyes for 40 years. We are asked to "Meet three boys," Ralph, Jack, and Piggy. We do not meet Simon at all. Piggy is Forster's hero, he is "the brains of the party," "the wisdom of the heart," "the human spirit," and as for the author, "he is on the side of Piggy." In a final bit of advice we are admonished: "At the present moment (if I may speak personally) it is respect for Piggy that is most needed. I do not find it in our leaders" (ix–xii). Actually, rightly understood, Piggy is respected all too much by our leaders, for he provides the means whereby they wield and extend their powers. Jack must steal Piggy's glasses to gain the power of fire. Forster, of course, was the arch-humanist of his day and apparently a subscriber to the "scientific humanism" Golding wished to demean. Contrast Golding's remarks to Jack Biles, a friendly interviewer: "Piggy isn't wise. Piggy is short-sighted. He is rationalist. My great curse, you understand, rationalism—and, well he's that. He's naïve, short-sighted and rationalist, like most scientists." Scientific advance, he continues, is useful, yet

> it doesn't touch the human problem. Piggy never gets anywhere near coping with anything on that island. He dismisses the beast . . . says there aren't such things as ghosts, not understanding that the whole of society is riddled with ghosts. . . . Piggy understands society less than almost anyone there at all.

Finally, Piggy is dismissed as a type, a clownish caricature who "ought to wear a white coat . . . ending up at Los Alamos" (12–14). He is the soulless child who adores the science that blew up the cities and obliterated the technological society he idealizes.

Putting Forster aside, we have in Golding's Jack, the lusty hunter who instinctively pursues power, a diminutive version of Huxley's ape. In the silence of the forest Jack hunts but is momentarily frightened by the cry of a bird, "and for a minute became less a hunter than a furtive thing, ape-like among the trees" (62). He meets his adult counterpart when the boys find the dead airman on the mountaintop: "Before them, something like a great ape was sitting asleep with its head between its knees" (152). And, in his hour of triumph, he looks down from his castle rock on the defeated Ralph and Piggy: "Power lay in the brown swell of his forearms: authority sat on his shoulder and chattered in his ear like an ape" (185).

In his last years Huxley came to a happier and more balanced view about the relation of science to the larger culture. His *Literature and Science*, published just before his death, is far more useful to writers on either side of that continuing debate than the heated exchanges of Snow and Leavis in the late 1950s and early 60s, and he avoids the overoptimistic prediction or projection of a "unity of knowledge" found in Edward O. Wilson's *Consilience* (1998). Though Huxley was mentor and guide for many of the ideas and devices that went into Golding's allegory, *Lord of the Flies* offers no real hope for redemption.[6] Golding kills off the only saint available (as history obliges him to do) and demonstrates the inadequacy of a decent leader (Ralph) who is at once too innocent and ignorant of the human heart to save the day from darkness. In later years Golding struggled toward a view in which science and the humanities might be linked in useful partnership, and he tried to believe, as Huxley surely did, that the visible world and its laws were the facade of a spiritual realm. He realized something of this effort in the moral thermodynamics of *Darkness Visible* (1974) and again, somewhat obscurely, in the posthumous novel *The Double Tongue* (1995). His Nobel speech asserts that the bridge between the visible and invisible worlds, one he failed to find in the earlier *Free Fall*, does in fact exist. Thus both novelists recovered to some degree from the trauma of disillusionment with scientific humanism suffered during the war, and both aspired to hope that humanity would somehow evolve beyond the old tragic flaws that assured the rebirth of the devil in every generation.

Note

6. In a letter to his brother, Sir Julian Huxley, 9 June 1952, Huxley counters the idea that there can be no redemption for fallen man:

> Everything seems to point to the fact that, as one goes down through the subliminal, one passes through a layer (with which psychologists commonly deal) predominantly evil and making for evil—a layer of "Original Sin," if one likes to call it so—into a deeper layer of "Original Virtue," which is one of peace, illumination, and insight, which seems to be on the fringes of Pure Ego or Atman. (*Letters* 635–36)

Immediately after their arrival on the island the boys embark on dramatic assertion of their masculinity in contradistinction to what they perceive as its 'other'. In the absence of girls or women, nature itself—announcing its untamed difference 'with a *witch*-like cry' (p. 7: my emphasis)—provides the otherness over which the boys attempt to gain control and establish their superiority. They set out to map the wilderness, casting themselves in the role of heroic explorers who confidently inscribe their presence on the island. In this contest, Golding suggests that the urge to dominate and the excitement derived from finding oneself in a position of power is innate to the boys, as his description of Henry, one of the younger children, demonstrates:

> Henry became absorbed beyond mere happiness as he felt himself exercising control over living things. He talked to them, urging them, ordering them. Driven back by the tide, his footprints became bays in which [the little sea creatures] were trapped and gave him the illusion of mastery. (p. 66)

The boys' tendency to set themselves off as controlling agents against an objectified, 'othered' world is not simply a gratuitous pleasure, but a highly functional (if catastrophic) element in a vicious circle of hierarchical self-assertion. While Henry is rejoicing in his rule over 'tiny transparencies' (p. 66), Roger starts throwing stones at him. Both boys are desperate to distract from their own helplessness and do so by projecting their fear of subjection onto an even weaker other. While bullying appears as a reliable strategy of expressing one's superior masculine composure, a self-conscious admission of fear would threaten their integrity as boys. . . .

As the boys' sense of forlornness steadily increases, so does their need for 'others' to testify to their masterful superiority. Their hunting of the pigs, for example, is clearly motivated by a desire for manly autonomy. The act of killing provides relief from their quintessentially 'feminine' and hence shameful feelings of fear and disempowerment, endowing them with the 'knowledge that they had outwitted a living thing, imposed their will upon it' (p. 76). Symptomatically, the killings become ever more ferocious and orgiastic, culminating in a particularly vicious attack on a sow. Beside themselves with fear, the boys fling themselves at this female emblem of their own panic and vulnerability, determined to master and kill it once and for all. As the sexual undertones and disturbing orgasmic imagery of Golding's description signal, this is no mere killing, but also a rape, which facilitates the boys' initiation into the violent masculinity of big game hunters:

> the sow fell and the hunters hurled themselves at her . . . Roger ran round the heap, prodding with his spear whenever pigflesh appeared. Jack was on top of the sow, stabbing downward with his knife. Roger found a lodgment for his point and began to push till he was leaning with his whole weight. The spear moved forward inch by inch and the terrified squealing became a high-pitched scream. The sow collapsed under them and they were heavy and fulfilled upon her.
> . . . Roger began to withdraw his spear and the boys noticed it for the first time. Robert stabilized the thing in a phrase which was received uproariously.
> 'Right up her, ass!' (p. 149f.)

The boys engage in a relentless, ultimately self-annihilating battle against their own nature. In their attempt to assert themselves as men and avoid the stigma of being referred to as 'a lot of cry-babies and sissies' (p. 90), they determinedly violate and destroy their 'femininity'. Willingly, they metamorphose into what they are not, donning impassive, uniform masks of masculine strength intended to bring about an eclipse of the terror of individuality. Jack's response to his transformation into a savage by means of clay and charcoal is typical: 'He looked in astonishment, no longer at himself but at an awesome stranger . . . the mask was a thing on its own, behind which Jack hid, liberated from shame and self-consciousness' (p. 69). Notably, the mask of savagery is so compelling and indisputably masculine that, while wearing it, the boys feel free to tie their long hair back for comfort, an act previously perceived as girlish and hence entirely out of the question.

The boys' masculinity is a precarious construct, extremely paranoid and hypersensitive to the forever imminent threat of unmasking. Both Piggy and Ralph become guilty of disrupting the camouflage by reminding the other boys of the actual reality of their condition. Piggy accuses the hunters of 'acting like a crowd of kids' (p. 42); Ralph refers to them as 'boys armed with sticks' (p. 138). The need to silence these voices of emasculation becomes an imperative necessity. Piggy's authority is easily discredited as his outward appearance and intellectual disposition stand in stark contrast to the boys' ideal of masculinity. Piggy is also the only boy who has enjoyed a practically non-patriarchal upbringing. With both his parents dead, Piggy, lives with his aunt whose authority he is never hesitant to invoke. '"Sucks to your auntie!"' and '"Shut up!"' are the other boys' unanimous standard responses to Piggy's female-authored rationality, whereas anecdotes of various fathers' heroic exploits never fail to find an eager audience. Piggy's deviation from the norm, his association with female (rather than male) authority, as well as his physical shortcomings, make him a paradigmatic candidate for ostracism. The boys quickly take to identifying themselves in opposition to him, whose deficient masculinity begins to function as a reference point for the suitability of their own conduct and appearance. Repeatedly, he is turned into 'the centre of social derision so that everyone felt cheerful and normal' (p. 164). The 'othering' of Piggy is finally complete when the pejorative epithet of his name is used to align him with the other victims of masculine self-assertion on the island. The answer to the question '"What would a beast eat?"' is '"Pig."—"We eat pig." "Piggy"' (p. 91). The boys' initially playful transformation of Piggy into an outsider becomes so effective that even in death they find it impossible not to compare him to something less than human: 'Piggy's arms and legs twitched a bit, like a pig's after it has been killed' (p. 200). In contrast to Piggy's, the 'othering' of Ralph is a slightly more difficult task that is eventually accomplished by associating him inextricably with his companion and chief adviser. During the boys' last assembly meeting, Jack tells both Piggy and Ralph to 'shut up'. Soon afterwards, he suggests to his hunters that Ralph is 'like Piggy. He says things like Piggy. He isn't a proper chief' (p. 139).

The boys' refashioning of themselves and their environment is driven by the imperatives of a masculinity based on negative self-assertion. This kind of masculinity endlessly produces and consumes 'others' against which its superiority is defined. At the same time, it enforces a total annihilation of the self's own inherent complexity, prescribing, instead of individual self-fulfillment, the ritual enactment of a tautly scripted role. The process of becoming a man within the conceptual framework of this particular kind of masculinity necessitates a complete surrender of the individual self to totalitarianist, effectively self-oppressive rules and modes of behaviour, hence propagating not self-liberation but ritual self-oblivion. Recoiling in terror from the reality of being frightened little boys on a desert island beleaguered by a world at war, the boys seek refuge in the security of ritualistic role-play. Ironically, in order not to lose face, they resort to gender-specific masquerade. . . .

As Peter Middleton argues, such an adamant refusal to apply 'the inward gaze' of self-inspection and self-examination is symptomatic of men's general inability to articulate and successfully negotiate their feelings 'for lack of a language for such reflection' (Middleton 1990: 3). Although the boys launch repeated attempts at discussing their communal quandary, their basic emotional inarticulacy remains conspicuous. Clearly the boys' failure to communicate how they feel stands in immediate relation to their eventual decline into violence. Even feelings of joy and delight are translated into a playful enactment of combat, accompanied by a shouting of linguistically unintelligible neologisms of pure, physical excitement: 'Ralph danced out into the hot air of the beach and then returned as a fighter plane, with wings swept back, and machine-gunned Piggy. "Schee-aa-ow!" "Whizzoh!"' (p. 12).

According to Middleton, seemingly innocuous boyish behaviour like this hints at a grave masculine dilemma. As his detailed analysis of boys' comics shows, the fundamental emotional inarticulacy of superheroes is an indispensable constituent of their 'hard', infallible masculinity, at once the cause and effect of their apparent invulnerability. Heroes act; they do not engage in discussions about how they feel. Heroes are free, independent agents, unencumbered by a complicated emotional life, maintaining their superiority by means of a glamorously costumed outward appearance and a compelling style. In most cases, their heroism is facilitated by an explicit negation of their private persona. For example, unlike Clark Kent, Superman appears incognito, reduced to an exemplary icon of efficiency and action. The public role of heroic masculinity categorically excludes the individual man's private self. As Middleton states, all that can emerge from such a state of enforced impassivity is 'the meaningless cry, pre-linguistic and therefore impossible to have a dialogue with' (Middleton 1990: 27). Golding's boys are clearly influenced by representations of superheroic masculinity and show themselves prone to emulate its rigidly coded behaviour in situations of particular exhilaration or distress. They are inclined to mistake the fantasy of heroism for something real, learning and acting out its scripts until their individual identities become indistinguishable from the roles they play. Hence, the boys' tendency to express their feelings by dint of pre-linguistic neologisms can be read as a symptom of their incipient metamorphosis into men, that is, their gradual hardening, and remote-controlled decline into emotional atrophy and self-oblivious role-play. . . .

As male violence and paranoia escalate in *Lord of the Flies*, one tends to become oblivious to the fact that Golding's protagonists are in fact boys, not men. All the greater then is the shock of recognition at the end of the novel when we are reminded that all of them—Ralph, Jack and Roger included—are in fact 'littluns'. Faced with the sudden appearance of grown-up *miles ex machina*, the hunters spontaneously drop their masks of masculine prowess and determination. Their self-assertive agency wilts immediately, to be replaced by an emotional display of feminine passivity and helplessness. A real man now occupies the superior position of masculinity that the boys struggled to usurp, an officer emblematic of the heroism the boys were so keen to emulate. However, like the boys before him, the soldier is only acting out a role, hiding his individual self behind a well-devised mask of 'white drill, épaulettes, a revolver, a row of gilt buttons down the front of the uniform' (p. 221). His fortuitous appearance saves Ralph and unmasks his persecutors, yet it does not resolve the novel's central problem. In fact, the soldier appears to epitomise the ordeal the boys have just been through, as he emerges from a world equally devastated by 'a jolly good show' (p. 223) of boyish 'fun and games' (p. 221).

Instead of effecting a genuine rescue of the boys from their gender-specific predicament, the officer only suspends it temporarily, delivering them back into the 'care' of the patriarchal order and its man-making imperatives that will eventually expect all of them to re-adopt the masculine role. Clearly, the officer himself has internalised all the imperative ideals of patriarchal masculinity: its mask-like uniformity, its paradoxical heroism-cum-servitude, its ethical ambiguity (this saviour carries a revolver!), and its peremptory unemotionality. The grown-up man's response to the boys' tearful display of despair and relief seems equally revealing: 'The officer, surrounded by these noises, was moved and a little embarrassed. He turned away to give them time to pull themselves together ... ' (p. 223). His masculine superiority expresses itself in a deliberate gesture of emotional detachment that serves to accentuate his own manliness in opposition to the boys' femininity. Moreover, his attitude of waiting for the boys to 'pull themselves together' is reminiscent of Jack's fateful earlier demand that the boys should learn how to 'put up with their fear'. The officer's appearance not only triggers the tears to which the boys succumb 'for the first time on the island' (p. 223); he also embodies the principle that is responsible for their tragic belatedness. . . .

Significantly, even at the very end of Golding's novel there remains some ethical ambiguity as to the goodness or badness of male violence. On being informed that two boys have been killed, the officer asks if the children are all British, insinuating that if the boys had been fighting against German or Japanese 'enemies', their savagery might have been acceptable. After all there is a war going on!

Lord of the Flies seems a far more complex and complicated book than humanist critics like Reilly, discussing an entirely hypothetical *conditio humana*, appear to find conceivable. Its message is expressly gender-specific, testifying to the urgent accuracy of Middleton's statement that 'modern men have suffered greatly in a series of wars generated by largely masculine codes of behaviour whose close examination might be a useful step towards preventing their endless repetition' (Middleton 1990: 2–3).

PAUL CRAWFORD ON HUMAN DEPRAVITY IN THE NOVEL

In *Lord of the Flies*, fantastic and carnivalesque modes are used to subvert postwar English complacency about the deeds of Nazism, particularly the Holocaust. . . .

Golding subverts . . . notions of racial and cultural superiority, of scientific progress, notions casting long shadows over atrocities against the Jews carried out in World War II.[7] He draws a parallel between the violent history of English imperialist adolescent masculine culture and the extermination of the Jews. . . .

Golding's critique is not directed exclusively at Nazi war criminality but at the postwar complacency of the English who too readily distanced themselves from what the Nazis did. He reminds them of their long infatuation with social Darwinism. Graham Dawson maps the trajectory of the "soldier hero," an "idealized," militaristic masculinity at the symbolic heart of English national identity and British imperialism. He argues that this "imagining of masculinities" in terms of warfare and adventure pervades the national culture, swamps boyhood fantasies, and, in particular, promotes rigid gendering, xenophobia, and racial violence.[9] In *Lord of the Flies*, Golding's critique of British imperial, protofascist history is powerfully registered by the Nazification of English schoolboys: "Shorts, shirts, and different garments they carried in their hands: but each boy wore a square black cap with a silver badge in it. Their bodies, from throat to ankle, were hidden by black cloaks which bore a long silver cross on the left breast and each neck was finished off with a hambone frill" (*LF*, 20–21). . . .

In *Lord of the Flies*, the world of the island is apprehended from the viewpoint of the schoolboys. Initially, they appear to be all-around empire boys, characters in the island adventure tradition that stretches back to Daniel Defoe's *Robinson Crusoe* (1719), Robert Louis Stevenson's *Treasure Island* (1883), and Ballantyne's *Coral Island*. But their preoccupation with natural phenomena and survival rapidly changes to a preoccupation with the unknown and inexplicable. They face beasts and phantoms in a succession of apparently supernatural events. Uncertain and fearful, the boys are subjected to unexplained phenomena. Suspense and hesitation as to the nature of the "beast" follow, and their fear increases accordingly. Although at first it is only the "littluns" that appear affected by this fear, the circle widens until all the boys, including Ralph and Jack, believe in the "Beast." The term *beastie* (*LF*, 39) quickly matures into "beast" (*LF*, 40). Initially, Ralph and Jack hedge their bets by stating that even if there was a beast, they would hunt and kill it. The mysterious disappearance of the boy who had seen the "snake-thing" compounds with the fall of snakelike creepers from an exploding tree and adds fuel to fear. In their beach huts the "littluns" are plagued with nightmares. And in pace with the growing sense of strangeness, the island environment itself becomes equivocal and menacing: "Strange things happened at midday. The glittering sea rose up, moving apart in planes of blatant impossibility; the coral reef and the few, stunted palms that clung to the more elevated parts would float up into the sky, would quiver, be plucked apart, run like raindrops on a wire or be repeated as in an odd succession of mirrors. Sometimes land loomed where there was no land and flicked out like a bubble as the children watched" (*LF*, 63).

Yet this strange transformation of the natural fabric of the coral reef is rationally explained by Piggy as a mirage. But such is the general uncertainty now of what is real and unreal that the fall of darkness is unwelcome. The equivocal nature of familiar things is constantly in view: "If faces were different when lit from above or below—what was a face? What was anything?" (*LF*, 85). . . .

Then Percival says he has seen the Beast and that "it comes out of the sea" (*LF*, 96). Thus, doubt and hesitation increase. Maurice says: "'I don't believe in the beast of course. As Piggy says, life's scientific, but we don't know, do we? Not certainly, I mean—'" (*LF*, 96). Then Simon amazes the older boys by admitting that "'maybe there is a beast'" (*LF*, 97). Here, Simon elliptically hints that the Best might be them: "'We could be sort of . . .' Simon became inarticulate in his effort to express mankind's essential illness" (*LF*, 97). . . .

With Piggy's murder, and the "pig hunt" of Ralph under way, clarification of the human nature of the Beast is intensified. The natural as opposed to supernatural interpretation of events is given its final and fullest exposition. Yet, even so, the uncanny does not completely override the supernatural. The pig's head remains strangely animated, as when the hunted Ralph strays upon it: "[T]he pig's skull grinned at him from the top of a stick. He walked slowly into the middle of the clearing and looked steadily at the skull that gleamed as white as ever the conch had done and seemed to jeer at him cynically. An inquisitive ant was busy in one of the eye sockets but otherwise the thing was lifeless. Or was it?" (*LF*, 204).

Effectively, the fantastic elements in *Lord of the Flies* operate in tandem with those of carnival: they combine to disturb us and subvert dominant cultural notions of the superiority of civilized English behavior. These are the kind of assumptions that buoyed the complacency of England, and indeed other Allied nations, namely, that the atrocities perpetrated by the Nazis were an exclusively German phenomenon. Within the fantastic framework, it is the break from potential supernatural explanation to the chilling and uncanny reality of natural explanation that disturbs us: that the Beast is human, Nazi-like, and English. We participate in the shock that this shift in perspective brings. Instead of externalizing and projecting evil onto objects, phantoms, and supernatural beasts, we confront the reality of human destructiveness. . . .

One of the most powerful carnivalesque elements in *Lord of the Flies* is that of the pig, which Golding uses symbolically to subvert dominant racial assumptions, in particular toward the Jews, and, universally, toward those humans considered alien or foreign to any grouping. This has alarming relevance to the atrocities committed against the Jews in World War II, yet has been overlooked by Golding critics who have not interpreted Golding's merging of the pig hunt with the human hunt, and the racial significance of eating pig flesh at carnival time.

The pig symbol is developed in *Lord of the Flies* as the pig of carnival time. It is a major motif: as locus of projected evil; as food for the schoolboys; as propitiation to the Beast; but more than anything, as the meat the Jews do not eat. This link between pig flesh and the Jews is reinforced by Golding's choice of the novel's Hebraic title. "Lord of the Flies," or "Lord of Dung," as John Whitley renders it, comes from the Hebrew word *Beelzebub*. As I noted earlier, Peter Stallybrass and Allon White argue that the eating of pig meat during carnival time is an anti-Semitic practice. It is an act of contempt toward the Jews for bringing about the Lenten fast. White asserts: "Meat, especially, pig meat, was of course the symbolic centre of carnival (*carne levare* probably derives from the taking up of meat as both food and sex)." That the pig becomes human and the human being becomes pig in the frenzied, carnivalistic debauchery of Jack and his totalitarian regime is important. The shadowing of pig hunt and human hunt, ending with Simon's and Piggy's deaths, and almost with Ralph's, signifies the link between the pig symbol and the extermination of those considered alien or outsiders. The name "Piggy" does not merely imply obesity. It is the lower-class Piggy who is always on the periphery of the group of schoolboys, always mocked, never quite belonging. . . . Piggy is alien or foreign, and, as such, he is a focus for violence based on the sort of racial assumptions found in Ballantyne's writing, but it is important to clarify the precise nature of his outsider status. The character name "Piggy" does not, unlike that of Ralph and Jack, feature in Ballantyne's *Coral Island*. Piggy is Golding's creation—a creation that suggests a Jew-like figure: "There had grown tacitly among the biguns the opinion that Piggy was an outsider, not only by accent, which did not matter, but by fat, and ass-mar, and specs, and a certain disinclination for manual labour" (*LF*, 70). We find something of the Jewish intellectual in this description of the bespectacled Piggy, with his different accent and physical feebleness. The stereotype of Jewish feebleness has been a stock in trade of anti-Semites and peddlers of degeneration theories.[19] It is here that we witness the anti-Semitism of carnival. In essence, Golding utilizes the imperial tradition of pig sticking to suggest a continuum between English imperialism and fascism. . . .

We may view Golding's use of carnival in *Lord of the Flies* as registering his deeply felt unease about the nature of English "civilization" in light of the events of World War II—of totalitarianism and genocide: a "civilization," among others, that is primed for the total wipeout of nuclear apocalypse. The misrule of carnival in contemporary history is presented as integral not simply to Nazis or other totalitarian regimes but also to England with its divisive and cruel class system. Golding lays bare an alternative view to civilized English behavior, one that counters accepted, familiar, erroneous complacencies. In the isolated focus, in the "carnival square" of Golding's island, carnival affirms that everything exists on the threshold or border of its opposite.[25] In effect, Golding explodes a Nazi–English or them–us opposition. . . .

Lord of the Flies subverts the view that the "civilized" English are incapable of the kind of atrocities carried out by the Nazis during World War II. These modes are deployed in the novel as an attack on what Golding deems to be a complacent English democracy, and its masculinity and classist attitudes in particular, in relation to the rise of National Socialism.

Notes

7. S. Laing argues that "the reversal of texts of high bourgeois optimism" in Golding's early work, and focus on the irrational, follows Golding's participation in and reflection on World War II. He refers to Golding's revelation of "history as nightmare" ("Novels and the Novel," 241).

9. See Dawson, *Soldier Heroes: British Adventure, Empire, and the Imagining of Masculinities*.

19. See Sander Gilman, *Franz Kafka: The Jewish Patient*. See also Gilman, *The Jew's Body*.

25. On the carnival square, see Bakhtin, *Problems of Dostoevsky's Poetics*, 128–29, 168–69.

MARK KINKEAD-WEEKES AND IAN GREGOR ADDRESS THE SYMBOLISM OF THE CONCH

Let us consider the finding of the shell, which provides the title for the opening chapter. We watch the conch, we might say, liberated from ordinariness, grasped, filled with meaning:

'What's that?'

Ralph had stopped smiling and was pointing into the lagoon. Something creamy lay among the ferny weeds.

'A stone.'

'No. A shell.'

Suddenly Piggy was a-bubble with decorous excitement.

''Sright. It's a shell! I seen one like that before. On someone's back wall. A conch he called it. He used to blow it and then his mum would come. It's ever so valuable—' . . .

The whole rhythm of this seems one of transformation—the unliving thing is disentangled and given a new social purpose. It announces man and summons men together, this 'Sound of the Shell'. As the novel proceeds this meaning becomes more and more sharply defined. 'We can use this to call the others. Have a meeting . . . ' It is his association with the shell rather than his size or attractiveness that makes the children choose Ralph as their leader; and having been established as the symbol of assembly, the conch becomes identified with its procedure, with democracy and the right to free speech. It becomes a symbol of immense suggestiveness. Every time a boy cries 'I've got the conch', he is drawing on the funds of order and democratic security. We take the point when Jack blows 'inexpertly', and when he lays it at his feet in rejection. The conch helps both to trace the trajectory of plot, and to establish character. Nowhere does Piggy's role seem more economically and poignantly expressed than when he prepares to confront the Tribe and its Chief with 'the one thing he hasn't got'. Then the conch in Piggy's hands becomes no less than the basic challenge to the Tribe to choose between democracy and anarchy, civilization and savagery. The answer comes in unequivocal terms: 'The rock struck Piggy a glancing blow from chin to knee; the conch exploded into a thousand white fragments and ceased to exist.' The shell, whose sound began as a summons to society, ends as a murderous explosion on the rocks. It traces out for us the swift tragic progress of the tale, and condenses its meaning—or so it seems.

But will this kind of reading satisfy, when we stop talking about the book from a distance and really look at the texture of the writing and the kind of experience it proffers? What will strike us most immediately is surely that the episode is far too long and circumstantial for any purely symbolic purpose. When we investigate the nature of that circumstantiality, what it reveals is Golding's concern to hold back rather than encourage the conceptualizing or interpretative intelligence. The counterpointing of the two boys shows this very clearly.

It is Piggy who is first excited by the shell, but only as a curio. It is Ralph's consciousness we live in, and he hardly listens to Piggy. Not one of the fat boy's sentences is heard to a conclusion. What is important about Ralph's 'day-dream', moreover, is that intelligence and social memory are laid asleep, while the physical senses, alone, remain sharply aware. Hence the description of fulcrum and lever, weight and resistance; the interest in how the shell is physically disentangled from the weeds. In fact the 'civilizing' intelligence is kept at bay while the actual conch in its strangeness and beauty is made real to the senses. Suddenly Piggy's babble stops, while he too strokes 'the glistening thing that lay in Ralph's hands', wet, reflecting light, strangely beautiful.

The second half of the scene elaborates the contrast. Now Piggy invents the idea of the meeting, giving the shell a social purpose; but again the life of the passage comes from Ralph, and he is only interested, as any schoolboy would be, in finding out how to blow it. Again Piggy moves into unison; the shell is primarily an object of play for both of them, and the simple vulgarity of the farting noises fills them with equal delight. The imagination at work is profoundly physical, and what it seizes is, precisely, the *sound* of the shell. It is made real to us in its context of salt water, brilliant fish, green weed; then in its own strange cream and rose spiral, embossed by an art other than the human; finally in the harsh otherness of the noise which shatters the peace of the island and terrifies bird and beast.

Physical realities come first for Golding and should stay first for his readers. Other meanings are found in and through them, as the man-breath passes through the shell's spiral to emerge as signal. But we must not translate the shell into the signal. What comes out is far from simple; and the human beings will be as taken aback as the animals and for the same reason. If we really look and listen, what we shall see and hear will be the harshness of human self-assertion as well as the signal of human sociability; will be the sound of irresponsibility and childishness as well as of forethought and intelligence; will be the fragility of order as well as the impulse towards it. As the sound penetrates the densest thickets, while clouds of birds fly and 'something squealed and ran in the undergrowth', man-sound prefigures stuck pig and stuck Ralph squealing and running for their life, as well as the assembly and the rules. Golding's symbols are not in fact clear, or wholly articulate, they are always an incarnation of more than can be extracted or translated from them. Even at this early stage, when the fiction seems to offer itself so alluringly for conceptual analysis, it is always richer and more profound than the thesis we may be tempted to substitute for the experience.

PAULA ALIDA ROY ON THE ABSENCE OF THE FEMALE IN *LORD OF THE FLIES*

William Golding's *Lord of the Flies* is peopled entirely by boys and, briefly, adult men. The absence of girls and women, however, does not prohibit interrogating this text for evidence of sexism/gender bias. We might begin by questioning the implicit assumptions about male violence and competitiveness that permeate Golding's Hobbesian vision. Today's sociobiologists will embrace these boys, whose aggressive reversion to savagery "proves" the power of testosterone-fueled behavior. In fact, one approach to studying this novel could involve research into the rash of books and articles about male violence, about raising and educating boys. Teachers might ask if or how this story would be different if girls had been on the island. Complementary books about girls include *John Dollar* by Marianne Wiggins, and *Shelter* by Joyce Anne Phillips. More interesting, however, is the text itself, in which the very absence of girls or women underscores how *feminine* or *female* stands in sharp contrast to *masculine* or *male* in Golding's island world.

The three major characters, Ralph, Jack, and Piggy, form a sort of continuum of attitudes toward life as it develops on the island in relation to their past memories of "civilized" British boarding school. Ralph and Jack are both masculine boys, handsome, fit, strong. Piggy, on the other hand, is fat, asthmatic, and physically weak. Jack, the choir leader, enters equipped with a gang; the development of this group from choirboys to hunters and Jack's deterioration from strong leader to cruel tyrant offer opportunities to look at male bonding and group violence, especially when we examine rape imagery in the language of the sow-killing scene. Ralph enters the book first, alone, and develops as the individualist who struggles to maintain some sort of order amid the growing chaos.

Piggy is the pivotal character: Not only do his glasses ignite sparks for the signal fire, but it is also he who defines the role of the conch in calling assemblies and he who insists on reminding the other boys over and over again of the world of manners and civility back home. Of the three boys, in fact of all the boys, only Piggy makes constant reference to a maternal figure—his "auntie," the woman raising him. We hear no reference to Jack's mother and we learn that Ralph's mother went away when he was very young. Some of the littl'uns cry at night for their mothers, but in general, only Piggy makes repeated and specific reference to a mother figure as an influence on him.

As Golding sets up the influence of Piggy's "auntie," we see that it is a mixed message about women. On the one hand, Piggy offers important reminders of civilized behavior and serves as a strong influence on and later the only support of Ralph in his efforts to keep order. On the other hand, Piggy's weakness and whining seem to be the result of the feminizing influence of his "auntie." He is, in fact, a somewhat feminized figure himself, in the negative stereotypical sense of physical softness, fearfulness, nagging. The early homoerotic connection between Ralph and Jack is underscored by Jack's jealousy of Piggy, his sarcastic derision of Ralph's concern for the weaker boy. Piggy's nickname, in fact, links him to the doomed pigs on the island, most notably the sow killed in a parody of rape by the hunters "wedded to her in lust," who "collapsed under them and they were heavy and fulfilled upon her" (154). The identification of Piggy with the slaughtered pigs is made explicit in Piggy's death scene: "Piggy's arms and legs twitched a bit, like a pig's after it has been killed" (209). If Piggy and the sow are the only female or feminized creatures on the island, then we can see that the one is useful only for meat and as a totemic figure and the other, the fat asthmatic boy, serves as scapegoat, victim first of ridicule, then physical abuse, and finally murder at the hands of the now savage boys under Jack's command. To the extent that he chooses to remain with Piggy, to hang on to elements of civilization, Ralph too becomes a hunted victim, "rescued" only by the appearance of the naval officer, Golding's ironic personification of adult male violence dressed up in a formal officer's uniform.

Searching the text itself, we find the female pronoun applied only to Piggy's auntie and to the sow. There are very few references to mothers, none to other women such as sisters or grandmothers. There is only one specific and direct mention of girls, quite late in the novel, when Ralph and Piggy and Sam and Eric seek to clean themselves up in preparation for a visit to Jack's camp where they plan to make a reasonable attempt to help Piggy recover his stolen glasses. Piggy insists on carrying the conch with them, and Ralph wants them to bathe: "We'll be like we were. We'll wash" (199). When he suggests they comb their hair "only it's too long," Piggy says, "we could find some stuff . . . and tie your hair back." Eric replies, "Like a girl!" (199). That single reference stands, along with the references to Piggy's auntie and the contrast set up by the absence of all other female figures, to identify the female with "civilization," ineffectual, far away, and dangerously weak. To return to the details of the rape-murder of the great sow, it is important to note that the sow is a mother figure, "sunk in deep maternal bliss," nursing her litter of piglets. The rape/murder of the sow and the final murder of Piggy suggest that the final movement into savagery involves the killing and defiling of the maternal female. Golding would not be the first to identify the female with attempts to control or tame male violence; he concludes that the female is unsuccessful because she is too weak, flawed, flesh-bound to overcome the ingenuity, craftiness, and sheer brutality of male violence.

Golding's Hobbesian view of human nature carries with it a whiff of misogyny or at least a suspicion that what women represent has little impact, finally, on culture or civilization. The island is a boys' club shaped by the theme of "boys will be boys" when left to their own devices. Obviously allegorical, the novel invites the reader to consider the absence of girls as a symbolic presence and the perils of ultramasculinity.

THEODORE DALRYMPLE REFLECTS ON HUMAN DEPRAVITY IN THE NOVEL

Lord of the Flies, by William Golding . . . was the first novel that caused me to reflect for longer than I read. . . .

Golding, who had been a naval officer during the war and had seen, indeed volunteered for, quite a lot of action, wrote the book because of the puzzle of evil. Where did it come from? We post-war boys knew perfectly well—it came from them, the enemy, the Germans, those who bombed London—but this was an answer that did not satisfy Golding. He had not only been a naval officer, he had been a schoolmaster, and knew boys. In the book, it is precisely Jack, the boy who leads the rest of the marooned children into the paths of unthinking evil, who says near the beginning of the book, "We're English; and the English are best at everything. So we've got to do the right things." He ends up as a tiny Hitler. So it could happen here after all.

A party of English schoolchildren are marooned without adults on a coral island. The aircraft in which they were being evacuated from a nuclear war (the proof that evil is well-established or ineradicable among adults) either crashed or was shot down. Ralph, an attractive boy with fair hair and physical grace, is elected leader, in part because he has found the conch that calls the children to order and that becomes a symbol of democracy among them: whoever is holding it has the right to speak. Piggy is first his acolyte and then his guide: fat, shortsighted, suffering from asthma, he is also his social inferior, as demonstrated by his grammatical solecisms (he says "them" for "those").

* * *

But unlike Ralph, he is capable of independent thought. Jack is the leader of the choirboys, who at the beginning of the book still have a distinctive uniform; he never accepts Ralph's leadership, rejects the symbolism of the conch, and in the end wrests the leadership away from Ralph, leading the choir and "the littluns" (the children too young to have individual characters) to the utmost savagery. Were it not for the intervention of a British naval officer, landing from a warship, at the very end of the book, Ralph would have been killed by Jack and his tribe of followers, who set fire to the entire island in order to flush Ralph out. This is a perfect replay of the German *Götterdämmerrung* ordered by Hitler: but the rescue by the naval officer is no solution to the problem of evil, since he himself represents the very forces that are making the nuclear war from which the children had to be evacuated in the first place.

Ralph and Piggy, though temperamentally very different and of two social classes, represent rationality and the rule of law. They want to act sensibly and responsibly; to build shelters against the rain, to light a fire and keep it going so that the smoke might attract rescuers. But Jack wants to hunt, and turns his choirboys into hunters; and in the end the dionysiac excitement of the hunters' life, with its bloody rituals and savage dances, comes to dominate, both by means of its intrinsic attractions and its ruthless imposition of conformity, leaving Ralph and Piggy isolated.

Jack and his hunters also offer the littluns protection against the "beastie," the imaginary creature they believe inhabits the island's jungle, that will come to destroy them in the night, in whose existence the older boys half-believe themselves. But there is no beastie, though an attempt to ward it off by erecting the head of a hunted pig on a pole acts to reinforce the belief in its reality.

Thus a band of British boys, when left to their own devices on an isolated tropical island (which, as Ralph points out at the beginning of the book, is a perfectly good island, because it has everything the children need to live comfortably—a Garden of Eden in fact) create a polity not very different from the Nazi one: obsessed with imaginary enemies, they invest a leader with total power, they suppress freedom, persecute dissenters and ruthlessly impose barbaric rituals. The last two to join Jack's savage tribe, the twins, Samneric (Sam and Eric), explain why they deserted the liberal-democratic Ralph and Piggy:

"—they made us—"
"—we couldn't help it—"

Precisely the argument of millions of ordinary Germans.

* * *

The book taught me a shocking lesson that I never entirely forgot, and that has been reinforced by my experience as a doctor in an English slum: that evil does not have to be introduced into the heart of man from without, it is always lurking within, awaiting its opportunity to take over, and we are never safe from its predations. There is evil within me, not because I am special, or specially bad, but because I am a human. The price of decency, one's own and everyone else's, is therefore eternal vigilance. The games we played—good us, bad them—were not true to reality. And in a brilliant moment, Golding captures the fragility of goodness, of the predictable, ordered social existence that I, like all my friends, led. At one of the assemblies, a "littlun," Percival, is pushed forward to speak by the other littluns.

> Piggy knelt, holding the conch.
> "Now then. What's your name?"
> The small boy twisted away. . . . Piggy turned helplessly to Ralph.
> "What's your name?"
> Tormented by the silence and the refusal the assembly broke into a chant.
> "What's your name? What's your name?"
> "Quiet!"
> Ralph peered at the child in the twilight. "Now tell us. What's your name?"
> "Percival Wemys Madison, The Vicarage, Harcourt St. Anthony, Hants, telephone, telephone, tele—"

Not only are we made aware in this passage of the cruelty of boys, who have no sympathy or empathy whatever for one of their own number, but the invocation, by a boy with an upper-class name, of an address suggestive of the safest, gentlest, most sheltered and prosperous way of life imaginable, is useless to ward off his terror. He then whispers that the beastie comes from the sea. Harcourt St. Anthony: geraniums, hollyhocks, thatched cottages, church bazaars, strawberries and cream for tea. But Percival Wemys Madison, so sheltered that he is unaware even of the social connotations of his name, ends up among the murderous savages led by Jack. The past can be destroyed.

Lord of the Flies, the first novel I ever thought seriously about, taught me that, because there is savagery in all of us, civilization is a thin and fragile veneer. I did not conclude from this that therefore civilization is bogus, for thin as its veneer might be, it is the only thing that protects us from barbarism; rather, its fragility means that it ought to be cherished and defended, while those who claim to despise it on account of its fragility do so either because they do not know how much they rely upon it, or because they are tired of always being civilized and want to revert to savagery.

* * *

The boy in the book with whom I had most sympathy was Piggy. Originally, this was because he was an outsider, an apparent failure, despised by everyone, as vulnerable as a hermit crab without its shell. It was how I felt at the time. His death at the hand of Jack's band of savages, who killed him because he was a moral reproach to them, was a terrible one, memorably described. He and Ralph go to confront Jack's tribe, who have stolen his spectacles to make fire with, and without whose one remaining lens he can hardly see at all. The tribe are ensconced in a natural fort, protected by a large boulder that can be rolled down on anyone who approaches it.

> Ralph heard the great rock long before he saw it. He was aware of a jolt in the earth. . . . Then the monstrous red thing bounded across the neck and he flung himself flat while the tribe shrieked.
> The rock struck Piggy a glancing blow from chin to knee; the conch [he was holding, the symbol of law and democracy,] exploded into a thousand white fragments and ceased to exist. Piggy, saying nothing, with no time even for a grunt, travelled through the air sideways from the rock, turning over as he went. The rock bounded twice and was lost in the forest. Piggy fell forty feet and landed on his back across that square, red rock in the sea. His head opened and stuff came out and turned red.

Piggy's arms and legs twitched a bit, like a pig's after it has been killed. Then the sea breathed again in a long slow sigh, the water boiled white and pink over the rock; and when it went, sucking back again, the body of Piggy was gone.

Death is unjust; death is unmerited; death is sudden; above all death is real and final; and yet one has to cope with it, to continue despite its dominion. That is what the passage taught me, a lesson reinforced by the death of a friend three years after I read *Lord of the Flies*. Piggy's death connected in my mind with his, and the pity of the two deaths coalesced.

Like Piggy my friend was shortsighted (I remember his blindness without spectacles, and the prominent, presbyopian bulge of his eyes); like Piggy he was asthmatic and couldn't run or play games. Like Piggy he was clever.

One day I went to his home after I had been away for two weeks. His mother answered the door.

"Haven't you heard? Michael died last week."

* * *

I thought of Piggy. In fact, though, my friend had died of his inability to breathe, and his heart gave out. The ambulance refused to come until the controller confirmed with the family doctor that the patient really had asthma, and he died shortly before it arrived. His death was not unconnected to human failing, the sadistic pleasure of the ambulance controller in his own punctilio. My friend's last words to his mother were, "I'm dying, I'm dying, can't you see that I'm dying."

Then his mother, a widow, said something terrible to me in the bitterness of her grief, and I never went back to see her as I think I should. She had another son who, unlike Michael, wasn't clever; he was a ne'er-do-well.

"Why couldn't he have died instead?"

I fled. What if my brother died, would my mother say the same thing? I was terrified. How complex, how difficult life was! Literature was the search for the sense of it. And desert island stories were my first intimation of its power. It could explain even where it could not change: though I think it changed me.

Peter Edgerly Firchow Examines the Implausible Beginning and Ending of *Lord of the Flies*

Though few critics have remarked on it or even noted it, there is something very odd about how the novel begins.[3] As far as we can tell, the boys have arrived on the island after their plane has been shot down at night by enemy aircraft during what seems to be part of a nuclear World War III. They were apparently being evacuated—much as English children had been in the early stages of World War II—from England and were being flown to safety in Australia (?) or New Zealand (?).[4] (Why all of this is never made explicit is a question that was left unanswered until Charles Monteith, Golding's editor at Faber, addressed it in 1986.) The novel begins on the morning after the plane has crashed, with one of the boys (it turns out to be Ralph) making his way out of the jungle by way of the "long scar" that the plane had smashed into the jungle as it crashed. He is followed a little later by another boy (Piggy), who emerges from more or less the same place and who has evidently been gorging himself on fruit. The two then engage in a contrived conversation about what occurred the previous night. Piggy first wonders what happened to "the man with the megaphone" and then about what happened to the pilot. Ralph asserts that there probably aren't any grownups on the island, something that seems to delight rather than distress him. He also claims that the pilot "must have flown away after he dropped us. He couldn't land here. Not in a plane with wheels."[5] He also thinks that the pilot will be back to pick them up. Piggy, however, is evidently more realistic and does not agree. He points out that the plane was under attack and went down in flames, with the cabin of the plane producing the aforementioned scar in the jungle as it crashed. To Ralph's question, as to where the remains of the plane might be, Piggy speculates that the plane was swept out to sea by the storm that was then raging, probably with some of the children (and of course the two adults) still on board (5–6).

Does all of this make any sense?

Not really. To begin with, it's very peculiar that neither boy—or, for that matter, any of the other boys who later join them, some of them from places quite distant from the site of the crash—has been injured in any way, not even slightly, nor has their clothing been torn or even singed or soiled. Jack's choir, for example, is fully dressed in caps and gowns.) What's more, there is no trace whatever of the plane that came down, except for the deep scar that it left behind as it smashed through the jungle. There is no detritus of metal, glass, propellers, food, tools, or weapons. There is simply nothing, not even corpses or body parts. Even if we accept Piggy's hypothesis that the plane was swept out to sea by the force of the storm, the fact that it has left nothing behind is very peculiar. Peculiar too is the circumstance that the plane evidently disappeared into the relatively shallow lagoon protecting the beach side of the island from the sea. The reef blocking the surf and the open sea is said to be "perhaps a mile away," which means that, no matter how great the force of the storm might have been, the plane could not have been swept out beyond the reef (8). (In fact, the storm was evidently not particularly powerful, since none of the trees on either side of the scar appears to have been blown down.) But if the remains of the plane are resting at the bottom of the shallow lagoon, then they should at least be visible from more elevated parts of the island and might possibly even be accessible. Such is, however, evidently not the case, for none of the boys ever mentions seeing the plane or, Robinson Crusoe-like, attempts to retrieve useful items from it.[6]

All of this is very curious. Curious too is what the point of all this mystery surrounding the boys' arrival on the island might be. It is clearly not due to carelessness on Golding's part, since, in speaking with Frank Kermode about *Lord of the Flies* in 1959, he said that "it was worked out very carefully in every possible way, this novel" (Kermode 1983, 201). Several years later, in conversation with Jack Biles, he reaffirmed his conviction that the novelist is a fully conscious craftsman: "I'm against the picture of the artist as the starry-eyed visionary not really in control or knowing what he does. I think I'd almost prefer the word 'craftsman.' He's like one of the old-fashioned shipbuilders, who conceived the boat in their mind and then, after that, touched every single piece that went into the boat. They were in complete control; they knew it inch by inch, and I think the novelist is very much like that" (Biles 1971, 177). These remarks obviously negate any supposition that Golding was simply unaware of what he was doing when he placed his boys on the island in so peculiar a manner. But if it was not an oversight or a blunder, then what? Certainly, all prior island fantasies, from *Robinson Crusoe* to *Peter Pan*, including Golding's explicit model, *Coral Island*, are at pains to show how their characters got there. Not Golding, however.

One possible answer might be to approach this apparently deliberate mystery from the perspective of the kind of philosophy that was current and most fashionable at the time *Lord of the Flies* was first published, namely, existentialism. Existentialism would account for the otherwise inexplicable way the boys "drop in" on the island by analogy to the way we have all "dropped in" on life—also an inexplicable and even "absurd" event. It's a given, in other words, which we simply have to accept without any further explanation, as with Martin Heidegger's idea of human beings being "thrown" into life. This existentialist answer to the problems raised by the strange beginning of the novel is admittedly an attractive solution to a difficult problem. It is especially attractive also because one of Golding's subjects of instruction at Bishop Wordsworth's School happens to have been philosophy, which presumably means that he would have been aware of existentialism even at this relatively early stage of its introduction into the English-speaking world. Still, I don't think it's the main reason why Golding arranged for the novel to begin as it did.

The main reason, I believe, is the utopian reason. Golding's intention is to establish, even at the cost of a drastic lack of realism, something like a laboratory situation.[7] Or, if lack of realism is too strong a phrase, then at least a "nonrealistic" laboratory situation, one, in other words, that is outside of, or more accurately, beside, reality. As he remarks in his essay on fables, "[t]he point of the fable under imaginative consideration does not become more real than the real world: it shoves the real world to one side" (1965, 97). Golding's aim in *Lord of the Flies* seems to be to set up the right conditions for an "experiment." Here, in other words, representative humanity (or at least representative male humanity between the ages of six and about twelve) is to be subjected to a "test," something rather like what the Hungarian critic Georg Lukács in his study of the historical novel calls an "extreme situation." Such a situation, though on the surface utterly atypical, is actually the most effective way of presenting a truly typical situation, since a more obviously "typical" situation would actually be "average" and therefore unconvincing. The very lack of realism, the very extremity of the situation, calls attention to the "experiment" that is being conducted in the novel. This kind of test or "gimmick," as both Frederick Karl and James Gindin call it (taking their cue from Golding himself), is also apparent in the ending of the novel, not only in its beginning. There a *deus ex machina* in the guise of a British naval officer, along with several members of his crew, steps ashore to "rescue" the boys. The way the book ends, in short, is quite as "absurd" and unpredictable as the way it begins.

Notes

3. According to Stephen Medcalf, however, high school teachers in Britain who use this novel to introduce their students to "high literature" for the first time "still rather irritably explain in answer to their complaints that we do not know how the boys of the story arrived" on the island. On the whole, it seems that the critics have shown rather less curiosity—or irritability, for that matter—in this respect than many high school students (2005, 12).

4. That the island is somewhere in the Indian Ocean is suggested by the intertextual reference to Ballantyne's *Coral Island*. However, it is also made clear in the novel itself that the plane must have been flying in this direction, since it is said to have made two prior stops in Gibraltar and Addis Ababa (17).

5. Readers of the published book could not have known that in the version Golding originally submitted to his eventual publisher

there were several planes rather than just one, and that these planes were equipped with detachable "passenger tubes" which could be released by the pilots to float down to earth on giant parachutes. These futuristic details were eliminated on revision, at the suggestion of Charles Monteith (Monteith 1986, 58). That Golding retained aspects of the original version (the distribution of the boys over various parts of the island, for example) while adding new ones (notably the "scar") makes the beginning of the novel confusing, apparently deliberately so.

6. None of these details seems to bother Mark Kinkead-Weekes and Ian Gregor, who simply assert that all the boys landed in a "detachable tube" which was then swept out to sea by a "great storm," together with some of the children on board. There is no discussion of why there are no injuries to the surviving children, or why some of them appear scattered over the island, or why there is a "scar" that has been caused by a plane crash (Kinkead-Weekes and Gregor 2002, 7–8).

7. Although, as we have seen, the original typescript version of the novel did provide more details about how and why the boys got to the island, Golding's revisions in the published version obscured those details, presumably deliberately.

Works by William Golding

Poems, 1934.

Lord of the Flies, 1954.

The Inheritors, 1955.

Pincher Martin, 1956.

The Brass Butterfly, 1958.

Free Fall, 1959.

The Spire, 1964.

The Hot Gates and Other Occasional Pieces, 1965.

The Pyramid, 1967.

Talk: Conversations with William Golding (with Jack I. Biles), 1970.

The Scorpion God: Three Short Novels, 1971.

Darkness Visible, 1979.

Rites of Passage, 1980.

A Moving Target, 1982.

The Paper Men, 1984.

An Egyptian Journal, 1985.

Close Quarters, 1987.

Fire down Below, 1989.

The Double Tongue, 1995.

Babb, Howard. "*Lord of the Flies.*" In *The Novels of William Golding*. Columbus: Ohio State University Press, 1970.

Babb sees many of the critics as incorrect in their focus on the meaning of the novel and in ignoring the novel's "artistry in narrative." To combat this perspective, he describes the narrative structures in the book, examines the characters, and using one scene attempts to show how "the method of the novel is realized in its language."

Baker, James, R. "Why It's No Go," *Arizona Quarterly* 19 (Winter 1963).

Baker disagrees with critics who categorize *Lord of the Flies* with works of Conrad or *Robinson Crusoe*. Instead, he comments on the influence Golding absorbed from classical Greek literature, especially Euripides' *The Bacchae*. Similarly, he points out that critics have too readily categorized Golding as being indebted to Christian sources and appearing as a Christian moralist. Instead, he suggests, Golding satirizes both the Christian and rationalist viewpoints.

Baker, James R., and Arthur P. Ziegler, Jr., eds. *Lord of the Flies* (Casebook Edition). New York: Berkley Publishing Group, 1988.

This book contains the complete novel as well as two interviews with Golding, a letter about *Lord of the Flies* by Golding's brother, and 12 essays, all but one of which were previously printed and some of which have been revised. The various writings explore psychological, religious, and literary views of the novel and compare the text to earlier Golding works as well as to other novels.

Biles, Jack I. *Talk: Conversations with William Golding*. New York: Harcourt Brace Jovanovich, Inc., 1970.

This book begins with a foreword by William Golding, reassuring us that what we are about to "overhear" are conversations between and among good friends who are curious about everything. The format involves brief exchanges on topics ranging from a particular character or work by the author to abstract topics like the nature of comedy, evil, and human intelligence. Most of the interviews are between Biles and Golding, but occasionally they expand to include British literary critic Frank Kermode and Golding's wife. This book is helpful for anyone interested in Golding's ideas and is accessible for beginning students.

Biles, Jack I., and Robert O. Evans, eds. *William Golding: Some Critical Considerations.* Lexington: The University Press of Kentucky, 1978.

The editors of this collection of essays assert that William Golding had—by the time of their preparations for the book—successfully established his stature as an author whose work would not diminish over time. Consequently, they determined that another work on the author by a single writer with a single perspective was not necessary and instead invited 14 literary critics to share their assessments. The original essays produced for this study cover large topics such as Golding's belief system as seen throughout his works, commentary on specific works, and some consideration of the technical aspects of Golding's style.

Crawford, Paul. *Politics and History in William Golding: The World Turned Upside Down.* Columbia and London: University of Missouri Press, 2002.

Crawford refers to his study of William Golding as a "properly historicized and politicized reading [that is] long overdue" (1). He looks at personal history and political context with the intent to give the novels a wider and more immediate context, one not limited to the perennial philosophical and moral issues of good and evil, suffering and guilt. Crawford points out that Golding was raised in a politically engaged family; his father was a Labor Party loyalist and his mother worked for groups promoting autonomy and freedoms for women. Golding published his first novel in the era following World War II and the Holocaust, and he joined with other writer/activists in protesting England's support of the American invasion of Vietnam. Crawford looks at Golding's novels and finds much that is concerned with specific and concrete political issues of the times, including class consciousness and conflict, the totalitarian personality, and the application of Marxist and socialist ideas to contemporary divisions of authority, privilege, and power.

Dickson, L. L. "*Lord of the Flies.*" In *The Modern Allegories of William Golding.* Tampa: University of South Florida Press, 1990.

Dickson points out four levels of meaning operating in the novel. First, there is the psychological dimension that shows Ralph, Jack, and Piggy as symbols of the three-part human psyche composed of the ego, id, and superego. Second, there are archetypal patterns—the quest motif and the Dionysian myth. Third, there is a reference to the two main characters who represent democracy and totalitarianism. Fourth, the novel serves as a moral allegory showing conflicts between good and evil.

Firchow, Peter Edgerly. *Modern Utopian Fictions from H. G. Wells to Murdoch.* Washington, D.C.: The Catholic University of America Press, 2007.

This scholarly book documents and examines the various manifestations in literature of utopian and antiutopian impulses. The author notes that utopian ideas have been mainly expressed in cultural and political contexts, but his focus is on the literary treatment of utopian ideals and their failures (dystopia) and the contribution these fictions have made to philosophical discourse about human nature and the possibilities for human community. In addition to *Lord of the Flies*, the author devotes a chapter to Orwell's *1984* and *Animal Farm*, H. G.Wells's *Time Machine*, Iris Murdoch's *The Bell*, George Bernard Shaw's *Major Barbara*, and general discussions of the ideas of Marcuse, Huxley, and Fukuyama.

Fisher, Jerilyn, and Ellen S. Silber, eds. *Women in Literature: Reading Through the Lens of Gender.* London and Westport, Conn.: Greenwood Press, 2003.

This volume contains 96 short essays, each dealing with a female character or characters or the absence of female characters in the most commonly read novels in world literature. A novel such as *Lord of the Flies* without a female presence is rare and significant, an omission with many and diverse implications. In addition to being brief, these essays are accessible and clearly written; the volume as a whole is a good introduction to the study of literature.

Gindin, James. "The Fictional Explosion: *Lord of the Flies* and *The Inheritors*." In *William Golding*. New York: St. Martin's Press, 1988.

Gindin addresses what many other critics have suggested about *Lord of the Flies*—whether it can be labeled a fable or assigned to the higher category of myth. Gindin compares *Lord of the Flies* to Golding's *The Inheritors* and states that both novels stand as unique works. He explains that from these Golding creates his own form, building on religious and literary tradition. Gindin calls the novel *Pincher Martin* Golding's "unique and symbolic literary explosion."

Johnston, Arnold. "*Lord of the Flies*: Fable, Myth, and Fiction." In *Of Earth and Darkness: The Novels of William Golding*. Columbia: University of Missouri Press, 1980.

Johnston looks at what he sees as the two connected but separate threads that run through the novel—the actual narrative that shows the boys becoming savages and the symbol of the beast that at first seems nothing more than an outgrowth of the youngest boys' nightmares and then comes to stand for the dark element that resides in all of them. Johnston admits that at times Golding is heavy-handed in trying to relay a message but believes this does not overpower the novelist's other skills as a fiction writer.

Kinkead-Weekes, Mark, and Ian Gregor. *William Golding: A Critical Study of the Novels* (Revised Edition). London: Faber and Faber Ltd., 2002.

The authors jointly wrote their first edition of this study in 1967 when Golding (who they knew and befriended) was still alive and had not yet written his final works. Their second edition (in 1984) was expanded to include commentary on the next three novels—*The Pyramid*, *Darkness Visible*, and *Rites of Passage*.

This third edition completes the work Kinkead-Weekes and Ian Gregor were to do, because Golding died in 1993 and Gregor in 1995. Kinkead-Weekes adds commentary on the last four novels—*The Paper Men, Close Quarters, Fire down Below*, and *The Double Tongue*. Also new for this edition are several pages of biographical material supplied by Golding's daughter, who took on the project of editing her father's journals.

Niemeyer, Carl. "The Coral Island Revisited," *College English* 22, no. 4 (January 1961).

While numerous critics compare *Lord of the Flies* to R. M. Ballantyne's *The Coral Island*, few do it as extensively as Niemeyer, whose essay is frequently cited by other critics. Not only is the comparison between the two novels made by critics, but it is made by characters in Golding's book as well. These characters seem to think highly of the Coral Island story, and at least one believes it is indicative of how humanity behaves. Ballantyne himself said it was a true story, and its pleasant characters and events starkly contrast to Golding's symbolic story of the boys' intrinsically bad selves let loose.

Rosenfield, Claire. "'Men of a Smaller Growth': A Psychological Analysis of William Golding's *Lord of the Flies*," *Literature and Psychology* 11, no. 4 (Autumn 1961): 93–100.

Rosenfield shows Golding's use of Freudian theory yet argues that the meanings of the novel are not so clear or simple. The book's goal, in her view, is not solely a re-creation of Freud's perspective that children are small savages rather than innocents. Beyond this, Rosenfield writes, Golding also comments on the adult world, itself damaged by war and dictated by irrational impulses.

Schoene-Harwood, Berthold. *Writing Men: Literary Masculinities from* Frankenstein *to the New Man*. Edinburgh: Edinburgh University Press Ltd., 2000.

This comprehensive study of the representation of masculinity in literature draws on both feminist theory and the issues raised in the new category of investigation known as men's studies. The first section deals with nineteenth-century representations, beginning with Mary Shelley's *Frankenstein*. In the second section, the author looks at four modern classics: *Lord of the Flies, A Clockwork Orange, A Room at the Top*, and *Look Back in Anger*. The third section examines the impact feminist theory has had on men's writing and men's representations of masculinity in literature. The fourth and final section is a reworking of older conceptualizations of masculinity from a gay male perspective. Although the subject matter in this volume is complex, it is also current and controversial and would be appropriate reading for beginning and advanced students.

Swisher, Clarice, ed. *Readings on* Lord of the Flies. San Diego: Greenhaven, 1997.

Swisher gathers together a large collection of essays on the novel, covering topics such as significant motifs in the text, its deliberately obscure setting, the use of irony, whether it should be categorized as literature, and its "unwarranted" popularity.

Contributors

Harold Bloom is Sterling Professor of the Humanities at Yale University. Educated at Cornell and Yale universities, he is the author of more than 30 books, including *Shelley's Mythmaking* (1959), *The Visionary Company* (1961), *Blake's Apocalypse* (1963), *Yeats* (1970), *The Anxiety of Influence* (1973), *A Map of Misreading* (1975), *Kabbalah and Criticism* (1975), *Agon: Toward a Theory of Revisionism* (1982), *The American Religion* (1992), *The Western Canon* (1994), *Omens of Millennium: The Gnosis of Angels, Dreams, and Resurrection* (1996), *Shakespeare: The Invention of the Human* (1998), *How to Read and Why* (2000), *Genius: A Mosaic of One Hundred Exemplary Creative Minds* (2002), *Hamlet: Poem Unlimited* (2003), *Where Shall Wisdom Be Found?* (2004), and *Jesus and Yahweh: The Names Divine* (2005). In addition, he is the author of hundreds of articles, reviews, and editorial introductions. In 1999, Professor Bloom received the American Academy of Arts and Letters' Gold Medal for Criticism. He has also received the International Prize of Catalonia, the Alfonso Reyes Prize of Mexico, and the Hans Christian Andersen Bicentennial Prize of Denmark.

David Anderson has been a lecturer in religious studies at Hertfordshire College of Higher Education in England. He published two books: *Simone Weil* and *The Tragic Protest: A Christian Study of Some Modern Literature.*

Kathleen Woodward was a professor of English at the University of Wisconsin at Milwaukee. In 1980, she published *The Technical Imagination* as co-editor.

Arnold Kruger is associated with the University of British Columbia.

James R. Baker wrote *William Golding: A Critical Study* (1965) and edited *Critical Essays on William Golding* (1988).

Berthold Schoene-Harwood is a senior lecturer in literature and cultural history at Liverpool John Moores University. She had earlier teaching positions at Swansea and Glamorgan and in 1995 published "Angry Young Masculinity and the Rhetoric of Homophobia and Misogyny in the Scottish Novels of Alan Sharp" in *Gendering the Nation: Studies in Modern Scottish Literature*, edited by Christopher Whyte.

Paul Crawford is a lecturer in mental health at the University of Nottingham. He is the author of *Nothing Purple, Nothing Black* and co-author of *Communicating Care: The Language of Care*.

Mark Kinkead-Weekes worked with Ian Gregor to produce two earlier works on the writings of William Golding. He and Golding were personal friends and discussed many of the ideas that were presented in the books. For the most recent and complete study of Golding, Kinkead-Weekes incorporated much of the earlier work of his colleague. He is also the author of *D. H. Lawrence: Triumph to Exile 1912–22* (1991) and *Samuel Richardson: Dramatic Novelist* and co-editor of *Tensions and Transitions, 1869–1990: The Mediating Imagination*.

Ian Gregor co-wrote with Mark Kinkead-Weekes two volumes about the writings of their friend William Golding. Gregor died in 1995, and his work was incorporated into the final and revised edition. Gregor also edited *Reading the Victorian Novel* (1980), was co-author of *The Moral and the Story*, and wrote of *The Great Web: The Form of Hardy's Major Fiction* (1975).

Paula Alida Roy teaches at Mohawk Valley Community College in New York. She is a poet, a writer, and a student/teacher evaluator. She has also published articles about teaching gender issues in *Overcoming Heterosexism and Homophobia* and *Women's Studies Quarterly*.

Theodore Dalrymple is the nom de plume for a British writer.

Peter Edgerly Firchow is a prominent scholar, now professor emeritus at the University of Minnesota. He is the author of *Reluctant Modernists, W. H. Auden: Contexts for Poetry, Envisioning Africa: Racism and Imperialism in Conrad's "Heart of Darkness,"* and *Strange Meetings: Anglo-German Literary Encounters from 1910 to 1960.*

Acknowledgments

David Anderson, "Is Golding's Theology Christian?" From *William Golding: Some Critical Considerations*, edited by Jack I. Biles and Robert O. Evans, pp. 2–4, 5–6, 16, 17, 19–20. Copyright © 1978 by the University Press of Kentucky.

Kathleen Woodward, "On Aggression: William Golding's *Lord of the Flies*." From *No Place Else: Explorations in Utopian and Dystopian Fiction*, edited by Eric S. Rabkin, Martin H. Greenberg, and Joseph D. Olander, pp. 219–20. Copyright © 1983 by the Board of Trustees, Southern Illinois University.

Arnold Kruger, "Golding's *Lord of the Flies*." From *Explicator*, vol. 57, no. 3 (Spring 1999): 167–69. Copyright © 1999 *Explicator*. Reprinted by permission of Heldref Publications (www.heldref.org).

James R. Baker, "Golding and Huxley: The Fables of Demonic Possession." From *Twentieth Century Literature: A Scholarly and Critical Journal*, vol. 46, no. 3 (Fall 2000) 311–27.

Berthold Schoene-Harwood, "Boys Armed with Sticks: William Golding's *Lord of the Flies*." From *Writing Men: Literary Masculinities from* Frankenstein *to the New Man*, pp. 53–54, 54–56, 56–57, 63–64, 64–65. Copyright © Berthold Schoene-Harwood, 2000. Published by Edinburgh University Press (www.euppublishing.com).

Paul Crawford, "Literature of Atrocity: *Lord of the Flies* and *The Inheritors*." Reprinted from *Politics and History in William Golding: The World Turned Upside Down*, pp. 54, 55–56, 58–59, 62, 63–64, 67–68, by permission of University of Missouri Press. Copyright © 2002 by the Curators of the University of Missouri

Index

Characters in literary works are indexed by first name (if any), followed by the name of the work in parentheses.